I0058156

Spa Business Marketing Strategies

Modern, Effective Online / Mobile Based Spa Marketing

Locate, Target and Get More Happy Customers

By Susan Fields

Visit www.SpaBusinessMarketing.com for MORE expert advice

Copyright and Trademarks

Disclaimer and Legal Notice

This product is not legal, accounting, medical or health advice and should not be interpreted in that manner. You need to do your own due-diligence to determine if the content of this product is right for you. While we have tried to verify the information in this publication, neither the author, publisher nor the affiliates assume any responsibility for errors, omissions or contrary interpretation of the subject matter herein.

We have no control over the nature, content and availability of the web sites, products or sources listed in this book. The inclusion of any web site links does not necessarily imply a recommendation or endorsement of the views expressed within them. We may receive payment if you order a product or service using a link contained within this book. BLEP Publishing or the author take no responsibility or will not be liable for the websites or content being unavailable or removed.

The advice and strategies contained herein may not be suitable for every individual. The author and publisher shall not be liable for any loss incurred as a consequence of the use and or the application, directly or indirectly, of any information presented in this work. This publication is designed to provide information in regard to the subject matter covered.

Neither the author nor the publisher assume any responsibility for any errors or omissions, nor do they represent or warrant that the information, ideas, plans, actions, suggestions, and methods of operation contained herein is in all cases true, accurate, appropriate, or legal. It is the reader's responsibility to consult with his or her own advisor before putting any of the enclosed information, ideas, or practices written in this book into practice.

Visit www.SpaBusinessMarketing.com for MORE expert advice

Forward

You've just opened your first spa and now you need to get the paying customers through the doors.

Firstly this book is NOT about how to run your spa on a day-to-day basis! You probably know how to do that better than anyone right now.

It is critical to your success that you get good paying customers straight away who will help you spread the word. These people are really the ones who will make or break your business and you then need to do everything possible to locate them and then to WOW them!

This book is specially designed to help you use the new revolutionary methods that are working right now and are highly targeted and highly effective to find and acquire these customers and then turn them into loyal repeat customers using low cost methods.

Using this book will probably be more useful than all the local press and flyers you can manage.

Would you like to use these new "under the radar" techniques to gain customers more cost effectively than any other form of marketing? They are so quick and easy even a marketing novice can do it.

Want a huge advantage over your competitors?

Would you like a massive advantage over your competitors right now to gain your first critical customers and to locate the ones that will spread the word?

Visit www.SpaBusinessMarketing.com for MORE expert advice

You want customers that will share their amazing thoughts and reviews of your spa with their friends.

Local marketing is of course very, very effective (and easy to get wrong if you don't know what you are doing) but I want to show you the blueprint that most spa owners don't know about.

Using it can highly increase the number of customers that locate you and want to experience your treatments.

Most techniques, once put in place, simply look after themselves whilst generating you new customers on a regular basis.

Much better than having to go out and conjure up new clients. This leaves you free to concentrate on your business and giving your customers that amazing experience so they come back to you again and again.

Making a profitable business for you whilst your competitors wonder how you do it. Is that something you'd like?

Would you like a steady stream of new customers?

You've probably already heard how much easier it is to sell to a current customer than it is to find a new customer.

You look after your current customers and I'll help you locate a steady stream of new ones thereby helping your spa to keep growing and become even more successful.

By creating great customer value you should get a fantastic lifetime customer generating good profits for you. Why would they want to go anywhere else when you give them exactly what they want?

When customers are happy with a service, they are reluctant to go anywhere else.

If you understand this principle it can allow you to do things that your competitors will think you are crazy to do.

But after reading this book you'll clearly understand how you can create a fantastic offer and experience plus make lots more money.

Making more money allows you to start dominating your spa market. You can enjoy better profits, a better work lifestyle, provide customers with a better spa environment whilst still outspending your competitors to acquire more customers.

It all comes down to a few techniques that I want to share with you in this book.

This one chapter is very important for you to understand. Fortunately for you - most other spa owners are not smart marketers.

I can show you how to do just that little bit extra and you will start to become the 'go to' destination.

This is great because it allows you to do things that they won't understand or realize the importance of. But by following some proven marketing methods you can be gaining valuable customers and increasing the value of your business simply because you followed the methods outlined in this book.

Criticism of this book?

The most obvious criticism is that this is not a specific spa business marketing book. Whilst that is partly true I have tried to give you *"specific examples and techniques directly useful to you as a spa owner"*. Most effective marketing ideas can be applied to various sectors. What works well in one sector often works in many sectors. Think of coupons. How many different businesses use them? From supermarkets, to garages, and what about rebates, birthday offers, invite a friend etc…I want to show you how to use these techniques in your spa business and use them really well so you beat your competitors.

Plus if I didn't target this book to you what are the chances of you finding a book specifically on increasing your business using step-by-step local marketing techniques? These are the techniques that are hard for the national and large regional companies to use. I want to give you every opportunity to do the stuff they can't.

Using the methods I show you – you can beat the competition and become very successful.

Plus I'm sure you want to know about methods that can be applied and used in your business right now if it helps increase profits and customers.

Use the blueprint that I give you here and you'll have a massive advantage over other local spa owners who don't follow these techniques.

In truth I doubt if 1 in 300 are doing everything I suggest here. Do just some of it and you should be well on your way. But you do have the opportunity to be the most recognised and highly regarded spa in your area.

It's all about getting a constant supply of new customers and then getting them to become good regular clients. Using the formula I'm about to show you this should become second nature to you.

Most are very easy to put in place and cost next to nothing. But all together they add up to a very powerful customer acquisition tool.

Want To Know Why Now Is The Best Time?

Gone are the days you could place a few adverts in the local press, and of course the yellow pages ad, and watch people arrive.

In some ways it's much better now because there are so many more ways to cost effectively target your customers.

Years ago your Yellow Pages advert was right next to all your competitors and there was very little to choose between you and them. Often customers just choose the largest ad figuring that they were the largest and more established company simply because their ad was larger!

With the local paper your advert only lasted a week and was not targeted in any way. You simply hoped that someone who saw your ad that week would call you and book an appointment. More often than not these ads just wasted money.

If you felt like showing off, you might have tried a few local radio ads. In those days people had to remember your name and address or your phone number. It was tough.

But now is the golden time to be using the proven methods detailed in this book. So many spa owners simply don't understand the power of the web to generate new customers.

They know they need a website and simply contact the local web design firm to put together a great looking site. But trust me web designers often know very little about creating a successful lead-generating machine. They want their work to look amazing and for you to say, "Wow that looks amazing".

Look at Google's homepage at Google.com – How fancy is that? Just a logo and a search box. Here's one of the most valuable companies in the world that tests everything.

They could have created a lovely homepage with all sorts of stuff but what worked best for them? Not some fancy design, simply a logo and a search box.

I'll help you create a customer gathering machine that can run almost on autopilot. You'll do stuff that will leave your competition wondering how you do it. Whilst I would love you to recommend us, I doubt you will. (Keep the secret to yourself. You don't want the competition to know this stuff – use it to your advantage!)

If this sounds good read on….

Here is what you can do

- Use Google and other search engines effectively to drive loads of customers to your door regularly.
- Use Facebook and other social media to target only those people interested in your offer
- Discover how a few simple 'Must Have' elements on your website can give you a huge advantage over your competition.

How Important is This?

How important is it for you to take time to understand this? It is vital!

Otherwise you'll discover a competitor who does understand it. Then you'll be powerless to act because you don't understand what they are doing and how to compete against them.

They could come in and dominate your local market because they know how to effectively generate new customers. Plus you'll have no way to generate an immediate cash pile if you need it. Don't let that happen. I can show you exactly what you need to do and give you the formula to implement it easily.

You know yourself how often you search the web for something you want. If you want a plumber you probably search 'town name plumber' look at their website and check out a few reviews, or you contact friends and ask for recommendations.

Long gone are the days when you look for the Yellow Pages and look for that ad. Things are different now. Even if you're buying gifts chances are you'll buy some online.

This book is specially designed to show you exactly what strategies to use in spa marketing. Use these simple step-by-step proven methods on how to gain customers, referrals and give your business the best possible chance of success.

Remember This

- This is your business and it has to make money.

I'm sure it's your passion and you want to help people. But unless you can pay the bills your dream is over. So spend some time and get the marketing right.

Even if you aren't interested in this part of spa marketing, I fully understand that. But read through this book. It's not a hard read and I can show you where and how you can get others to do this for you. But it would help if you had an understanding of it.

You need to devote your time to the activities that can increase your business.

Remember - You can't increase the business if you are doing a massage.

Now I'm not suggesting you want to be the next Donald Trump or Richard Branson. But remember that Richard Branson doesn't fly his own planes and Donald Trump doesn't lay the bricks. But they do both have a formula in place so that their business runs, (even if they are on holiday) generates profits, and gains new customers.

Their experience is in doing the profitable stuff of growing their business and that is what you need to do. Focus on the activities that bring in the money at least at the start.

Table of Contents

Visit www.SpaBusinessMarketing.com for MORE expert advice

Visit www.SpaBusinessMarketing.com for MORE expert advice

13

Visit www.SpaBusinessMarketing.com for MORE expert advice

Here's Exactly How To Design an Automatic Customer
Generating Website That Works 24/7 and Does 99% of the
Work For You - Easily...

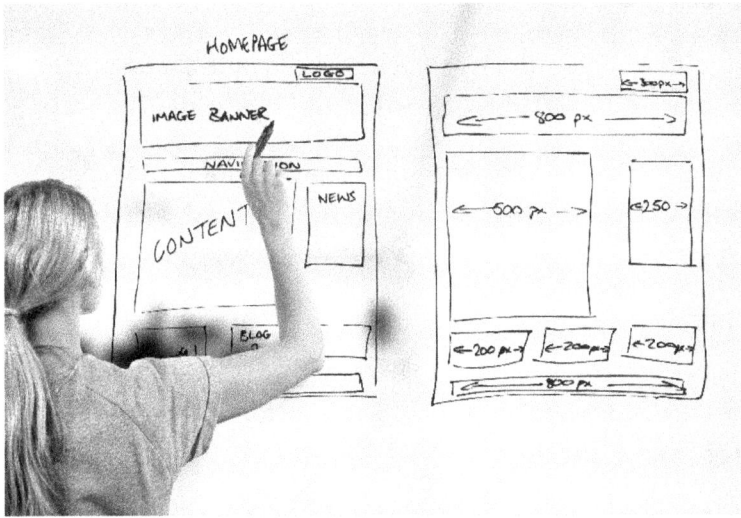

If you had set up your business 20 years ago you would never
have had to consider building a website. But in 2014 it's a
'MUST'. You simply have to do it. All your competitors will have
their websites and you need one, too.

But the good news is using the methods and techniques I show
you here you can get a great customer gathering machine that
runs on autopilot.

Where as a competitor's website might look better, you've used
the strategies revealed here to create a website that does what it
should.

I don't care if you hate the web, don't know the first thing about
building a website, don't like computers. Simply put, your
customers expect to find you on the web.

The best bit is that it can be really easy to get your website up and running. I remember years ago I worked at a company that wanted a new website built for one of their products. They only needed about 15 pages including a few graphics and video. They were quoted just over $22,000.

Even now if you select the wrong company you'll easily pay a few thousand dollars for a relatively simple website.

If you contact a local web design firm chances are they'll charge you thousands. Now when you are starting up cash is tight (and even if it isn't you'd be silly to pay more than you should).

TIP - This is what you need to understand. The prettiest website may not be the best. It's all very well saying you want flashing graphics and video – but is it what your customers want? Are you sure?

If your customers come across your website at work do they really want your movie playing across a quiet office? Chances are they'll close your website in a heartbeat!

Also if you let a web designer create your site, they'll probably give you a great looking website and you'll think it's just amazing. It looks fabulous BUT being good looking and useful are two different things!

You'll want your website to do a few functions:

- You need to capture a person's email address. It is vital. (Why? Please read the Autoresponder Chapter.)

- You need to showcase your spa and the treatments you offer with full details on each.

- Customer Testimonials are very important to demonstrate trust and quality.

- Online booking if you can.

- Where your spa is located.

- Frequently asked questions

- Contact form (helpdesk)

But before we go any further there are 2 things you need:

1 – Domain Name
2 – Website Host

Domain Name – this is what people type in so they can reach your site directly e.g. Amazon.com, Ebay.com.

They only cost a few dollars and I highly recommend

GoDaddy.com.

They are one of the largest domain registration companies in the world and their prices are highly competitive.

What domain should you choose?

You should register the name of your company e.g. "WellnessSpa.com" or "SallysSpa.com" but now that domain might not be available as some other company may have registered it.

Here you have two choices. Take a look and see if there is actually a website on that domain. Often people buy domains and then decide not to use them.

If that is the case you can use www.WhoIs.net to find out who owns the domain and contact them and see if they wish to sell. Often you can buy the domain for just a few hundred dollars.

You'll want to use the .com version or your country code e.g., .co.uk if you are based in the UK.

If your first choice is taken and you can't buy it, you need to decide if you want to register the .net or .org version (for country domains I would not use lesser domains like .org.uk because your customers will never remember the correct ending) even using .net or .org a lot of your customers will assume it's .com and go to the wrong site which is not good for business!

So what can you do?

You could use something like "SallysSpaTownName.com" or "SallysSpaRelaxation.com".

TIP – I would also strongly recommend that you register your "Spa + Your Area Name.com" If you live in a town called "Chertsey" try and register "ChertseySpa.com" if that is not available you could try "SpaChertsey.com". This could really help in the future to get your website found in Google.

If you can buy BOTH your CompanyName.com and Spa+TownName.com You can set them so they BOTH go through to the same website.

INSERT FORWARDING BOX

You want to get your Spa+Town.com hosted by a web host (recommended below) and then forward your company name on. GoDaddy makes this process easy.

That way on all your business cards and leaflets you can put your companyname.com and when someone types it in it goes to your website.

Having spa+townname.com will make it easier to rank in Google, and after all, you want to be higher in the rankings than your competitors. So any little boost you can get will help.

PLEASE NOTE – Buy only your domain through them. I would not use them to host your website.

Personally I use a company called BlueHost.com.

I have found them to be fantastic and do everything I need. Again I highly recommend them. I'm sure you'll be able to find hosting for a few dollars cheaper if you search around, but trust me it's really not worth it. A few dollars saved could easily be outweighed if your website goes down and is not available or they let you down with poor support.

I think their hosting is only about $5 a month anyway and they have everything you'll need to have a fantastic website.

Their basic package should easily be enough for you to start with. You can always upgrade later. But even the cheapest package includes everything you'll need to have a great looking site.

Plus by signing up with them you'll get a free Google Adwords voucher worth about $100 – that entitles you to a $100 free advertising on Google which is great. I'll explain more on that later.

Your Website Design

Now is the time to start imagining what you want on your website and get ready to blow the competition away. It's worth spending some time doing this right because it's probably the first impression a potential customer will have of your business. So it needs to be done right.

I've already given you a basic list of what you need on your site. But now is the time to put all that together. Don't worry about this you can do it all easily and cheaply without any technical knowledge.

I've run a seven-figure business online without knowing any code. You really don't have to if you follow my methods.

How To Make The BEST Website – Step 1

First you want to visit as many competitor sites as you can locally, nationally and even internationally. Make a list of everything that you like and just as important everything you don't like (and what sites you saw those features on).

Try and put yourself in your customers shoes and think about how easy it was to find certain information on a website. If you find one site that has particularly easy navigation e.g. you can find what you want without having to search hard for it, just make a note.

Also think about what colours work well.

What type of photos work best,? Do they include people or just buildings? Do they use videos? If so, what's on the videos?

Notice how they use testimonials and generate trust.

What information do they give? What are they missing that you wanted to know?

Sometimes its worth paying more attention to the national brands, because hopefully they spent a bit of money on testing and tracking their website so they know what works best. This isn't always the case but worth thinking that some do. So if you see particular elements just ask yourself why they are there, and can you use the same ideas?

Spend time doing this. The better your list the better your site will end up being.

Step 2

- Next ask yourself, "How can I improve these elements even further? What can I do that will make us stand out?"
- Why should someone pick us rather than a competitor?
- What 'Wow' factor can I give customers?

Hopefully now you have a fantastic list of what you want and a good idea on how your site will look.

You should also have a list of the stuff you love and the websites you found them on, plus a list of things you don't like.

Just a note – don't go against basic website rules.

- Customers will expect to have your logo in the top left corner.
- Navigation links need to be along the top or left column. NEVER on the right or Bottom (you can repeat a few navigation links at the bottom)!
- Any shopping cart buttons should be top right e.g. buttons that allow you to view your cart or checkout.
- Address, Contact Details, Terms etc. at the bottom of the page.

Since they are in those positions on 99% of all other sites people are trained to look in those areas for those objects. Don't make them look hard for information or they will leave your website fast!

So How Do You Design Your Site?

This is where the novice can end up spending thousands. But following the steps below you can get exactly what you want for a fraction of the price you might pay a local web design firm.

You really have 2 choices.

- Use a website called 99Designs.com

This is a great website where you post a project detailing exactly how you want your website to look. You give as much information as possible. You then set the price of what you want to pay.

Over the next few days you'll get designers from all over the world submit their designs for your website. Within a week you should have loads of possible designs and you simply pick the one you like best.

They'll then give you the design and the files to give to your programmer (see step 2) to put together into a working website.

Or if you are completely happy that you can communicate to a designer / programmer how you want your website to look and work simply go straight to

- Elance.com

This site works similar to the site above in that you post a project detailing exactly what you want and giving as much information as possible. The more detail, the better quality bids you'll receive.

When you submit the project I would choose 'fixed price' rather than an hourly rate. That way you have a guaranteed price.

I would also pay the $25 to have the projected 'Featured' especially as a new customer to Elance it will give your listing more creditability and show that you are serious.

Think about it from a provider's point of view – they see hundreds of listings from new Elance customers like you. They'll spend time putting together a proposal and find the project isn't awarded to anyone. So they certainly favour highlighted projects because it shows you are serious.

After you have submitted the project you'll then have people bid on your project saying that they can do what you require for a set price.

Also once you have posted the project I would invite as many providers as you can. The more bids you have the more information you have to choose the best provider.

So you could get your super new website all set up and working for just a few hundred dollars. The only thing you'll need to do is write the content since you know exactly what you want to say. But I would expect that you'll pay about 70% less on Elance than you would if you went to a web design firm in the local town.

Plus remember Elance for the future because it's not just for website programing. You can get people on there to do almost anything you require for your business. If you need leaflets or business cards designed that is the place to go. You can ask them to carry out research.

Almost anything you need doing that you can't or don't want to do yourself outsource it so you can focus on the important stuff of getting customers booking.

Just a TIP on Elance so you get the best possible bids.

- When you sign up verify your credit card with them.
- Spend the $25 and make your project 'Premium'.

So often people will post projects on Elance and then not follow through or award it. By verifying your card and posting your project as premium anyone bidding on your project will know you are serious.

In return you'll probably get better and more bids. The more bids you get the better your options of choosing a provider you are happy with.

Personally I wouldn't use any provider who doesn't have any feedback. It's your choice but I have been stung before and I have found new providers "all keen and promising the earth and then simply failing to deliver". I'd like to see feedback of at least 10+ clients and there are thousands of providers who have that.

Big TIP - The other thing I often do is write in my project posting usually towards the bottom of the description, "Please write 'happy days' at the top of your bid so I know you have read and understood this project."

You'll be surprised at how many providers just bid without fully reading a project. This way you can quickly discard all those who didn't read your project fully.

You'll then have a list and you can start looking at their feedback, asking them questions, etc. See how they respond and decide with whom you would like to work.

Once you've award the project you'll want to break your project down into various stages with a time frame. Use the Elance Escrow service so your payments are protected.

Often projects would go something like:

- Start – 20% (paid and released to the provider upfront)
- Basic set up and content 20%
- Autoresponders, videos all set up and working 20%
- Completed 40%

If you pay a provider in stages it works for them and you.

Try and load the payments towards the end of the project. Otherwise you might find your provider does the easy work, takes the money, and then unfortunately becomes ill!

Yes you'd be surprised at how unlikely some providers are!! Often they get ill or have major unforeseen problems!

Your project completion will almost certainly be a little later, but that is why working with a provider that has a lot of good feedback you can start to eliminate some of these issues.

Make sure you are "Responsive"

When you post your project tell them you want a 'Responsive' website. This is becoming more and more important. It basically means your website will automatically change depending on if someone is searching for you via their PC, tablet or mobile phone.

Your website will still look correct and Google should give you more visitors from those devices than websites that are not set to display correctly, especially tablets and mobiles. This will help you massively in Google maps and local listings.

Important - Make sure your website is not using 'Flash'. If you don't know what it is that's fine (it allows some fancy stuff on websites) BUT search engines find it very hard to understand, iPhones and iPads won't display that content (therefore a lot of users simply won't see your website and you'll be wasting money on advertising) and it slows your website up.

Also don't use small fonts – there are no space issues on the web. Make it easy for your customers to read. Black text on a white background is perfect.

Break up paragraphs into small bite size chunks. Probably only 2 or 3 sentences are fine. Kind of like this! It makes it easier to read (ignore what your English teacher told you!)

It's more important that people read and understand what you have written than it is to use perfect grammar. People tend to scan the web rather than read big chunks of text.

Important TIP - You need to do everything you can to make it easy for them. Don't make your visitors work; make it easy for them.

Speed is a big issue as well. Your website needs to load quickly and you'll get bonus marks from Google the faster your website is. Tell your provider you want all your images 'optimized'.

They'll know what it means and it can reduce the time it takes images to load by optimizing them. It takes out some of the colour and pixals and yet your eye won't notice the difference.

Tell them that it needs to be WC3 compliant (again don't worry about it, it just means the code they write must be clean and correct.) It helps in Google as well.

Your images must use 'alt tags'. For each image you give your provider tell them what the alt tag is "and then in a few words describe what the image is".

A few alt tags on each page (a few NOT all) should contain words that are associated with that page and your business e.g. "relaxing massage" "spa treatment".

You also need to give each page a title tag. This is generally what Google will display in its search results as the blue heading

```
<head>
    <meta http-equiv="Content-Type" content="text/html; charset=UTF-8">
    <!-- InstanceBeginEditable name="doctitle" -->
    <title>Foxhills Health Spa - luxury resort,spa and health club in Surrey</title>
    <meta name="keywords" content="health spa, spa, spa hotels, spa retreats, spa resorts, health spa club,
packages, spa finder, luxury spa hotels, thermal spa hotels, family holiday spa,"/>
    <meta name="description" content="Health spa hotel and retreat ideal for a relaxing, luxury spa break
    <meta name="author" content="Foxhills"/>
```

It should be no more than 50 to 60 characters and if possible start with your most important keywords (the words that if someone typed into the search engine you'd like you spa to appear under).

Then you also need to write a description for that page that is no more than 150 characters.

Again use your important keywords. But DON'T just repeat the words and make sure they reflect the content that is actually on that page.

These tags will be different for every page on your website.

BIG TIP – Try and use a Title and Description Tag that would want to make the visitor click on your listing. Can you include a bonus offer – or something to entice the user to click your listing rather than a competitor's?

Once you have the click to your site you have the chance to make the sale that your competitor doesn't because you took the time to create a few great sentences!

E.g. What would you prefer to click on if you wanted to be found for the phrase "Spa treatments in Chertsey"?

Your site:
Title: No1 Spa Treatments in Chertsey with Free Oils

Description: Receive a wonderful spa treatment in Chertsey, relax and enjoy and receive a complimentary bottle of massage oil to take home.

Or your competitor (who doesn't know what they are doing!)

Title : Sallys Spa Room

Description: Our spa rooms were found in 1980 and we have provided massage treatments in Chertsey ever since.

The next important element of your webpage is the h1 tag. This is basically the headline you'll use on the page. Google will likely decide that this is what the page is about. It is one of the most important elements on the page.

Your h1 tag /webpage headline again should use your most important keywords (but again describe the page). They can be the same as your title tag if you wish but you'll probably want to expand it a bit e.g. "NO1 rated Spa Treatments in Chertsey. Receive a Free Bottle of Deeply Relaxing Massage Oil Worth £25 With Every Treatment Booked By..."

You can have other sub heads on your page ranging from h1 – h6. But really you should have only one of each and most pages will probably only use h1 and possibly h2.

You then need LOTS of RELEVANT content!

Simply Put - Google loves great quality content.

Write as much as you can, but make it interesting.

So give Google what they want and hopefully in time you'll be rewarded with great rankings. Better rankings should equal more customers that you didn't have to pay for advertising on – therefore making them much more profitable.

If you follow the advice above and can get ranking in Google for your place name and spa or spa treatments e.g. Chertsey Spa or Spa Treatments Chertsey you should get lots of free customers.

If your competition needs to pay for adverts because they didn't follow the steps above that make you more profitable and allow you to invest more in your business, then they can.

Another thing to remember is search engines try and track what their customers do. So if Google shows your result for the term 'Reading Spa' and the visitor clicks on your site but for whatever reason clicks straight back to Google, Google thinks, "Oh that can't be a great result for that term 'reading spa'." If this pattern is repeated over and over Google will think you are not relevant for that term.

So the design and ease of use of your website is important. Google knows if you get repeat visitors and they like that because it shows them you have useful content. Also if a visitor stays on your site for 10 minutes before clicking back and researching Google, they think wow that customer must have like that site. If that is repeated you'll get a boost.

So give your customers what they want – great relevant content and capture their details so you can follow them up. Video can

33

help increase the amount of time people spend on a page. But try both and make sure video is helping you.

Project Summary – Posting your project

- Must be a 'Responsive' website
- Be WC3 compliant
- All images must be optimized
- No flash

Your website must:

- Use title tags
- Have great description tags
- Use image tags
- Possess great content
- Break content up into easy to read sections, with subheaders

Here's The Secret To Gaining Customers and Getting Them To Do What You Want....

Collect Their Email Address - Here's how to do it really effectively!

Now that you have your all singing all dancing totally mind blowing website that is making your customers sit back and go 'wow' I must use these people, you need to start capturing their details so you can contact them easily in the future anytime you want (and almost for free!)

- You could contact them to offer various special offers during your quiet times
- To let them know about new treatments
- Ask them to tell their friends about you
- Simply remind them about your services

The easiest way to do this is use an email sign up form. A box on your website that allows customers to enter their email address.

Sadly however I would expect less than 1% of people to do that – Why? Because they know entering their email address will probably result them in them receiving spam emails (which of course is not going to be the case with you) but they don't know that.

Following up with customers is vital (as you'll see in the Autoresponders chapter). So how can you greatly increase the chances of your visitors giving you their email address?

Simply put, you want to bribe them!

Yes you want to give them an offer presented in such a way that they think the benefits outweigh the chances of receiving a load of junk emails.

So you want to make them an offer they can't refuse. The better the offer the better your chance of capturing their email address and then of making a sale. Without capturing their email, making the sale later will be much harder.

Think of it this way. If you're offer said, "Enter your email address and I'll give you FREE spa treatments for a year", how many people will join? Probably everyone since your offer is so good.

Compare that to a form that says, "Enter your email address here". How many would sign up?

Here's exactly what you should do

So come up with an offer that is hard for your customers to say no to. Personally I'd try and stay away from discounts. You don't really want your customers to come to expect discounts (after all it hurts your profits as well).

One thing that is popular on some sites is to give away a free report. Something like "Discover the Top 12 Things Health Spas Don't Want You to Know" or "7 Quick and Easy Step-by-Step Tips You Can Use to Make Yourself Look 8 Years Younger". You could go back to Elance to get someone to write these for you. Create something of interest to your customers, something they want to read and will give their email address in exchange for.

Or you could go down the route of offering a "Free 15 minute spa treatment". I don't know if that is possible. But if you could offer some bonus like that you'll get the people who are really interested.

Plus once they come to visit and try you, your chances of making a bigger sale later are hugely increased.

Have a think of what you can offer in exchange for their email address.

How to capture MORE email addresses

Now it's fine to have a little sign up box on your web page with that offer but I would strongly, strongly suggest that you use what is called a pop up box.

That means when a visitor comes to your website this box pops up on their screen with your offer asking for their email address.

Even better is a pop up light box which means when the pop up loads the rest of the page goes darker so it really stands out. That makes the customer either give you their email address or close the box.

Now I know you hate pop up boxes; chances are your customers probably do as well. But great marketing sites use them because they WORK. Providing you give your customer a great experience it's fine.

You'll find a good offer on a website will probably only get 1-2% of people entering their email address. A good offer using a pop up can easily get 20+% of visitors.

You can get these pop up boxes from Aweber.com. They have some preset templates. Or go to Elance and get someone to design one for you.

On your sign up box it's worth putting (provided you don't) "We do not share or sell your details with anyone". That one line can help increase your sign up.

Let Me Show You How Important This Is...

Let me give you an example: Say you get 5,000 people to your website over one month:

- A poorly designed email sign up form lower down your webpage gets only 5 email addresses.
- A great offer with a form higher up on the page gets 65 email addresses.

- A great offer using a pop up gets 1000 email addresses.

Over the year the total email addresses are:

- Poor quality offer = 60 email addresses
- Better offer = 780 email addresses
- Light Box pop up = 12,000 email addresses

Remember these are highly qualified visitors who ALL expressed an interest in your product.

What list do you think has the best chance of making more sales and getting more customers?

Which list would you like to own?

Yes we hate pop up boxes but in this instance if done probably they can work incredibility well and provide you with a powerful marketing tool that makes your business worth more.

As you get more familiar wth your site, you can start generating offers and refer people to what we call a 'Squeeze Page' that is a page where the only option is to enter your email address or leave. Some of these squeeze pages can get more than 40% of people opting in!

Take a look at www.SpaBusinessMarketing.com for an example of what these pages look like. They are designed for just 1 thing – collecting email addresses and giving something in return.

As a side note you could start using these highly targeted lightbox ads to target your competitors. I'm guessing you might not be the only spa in your area.

Advanced stuff

You can register another website domain e.g. "AmazingSpaOfferForTownName.com", put up a website and only bid on your competitor's names.

So if someone types your competitor's name into a search engine they'll see your ad (you can target more than 1 competitor, just enter them all and send them all to the one page).

Send them to a page that has an incredible offer (remember these are people who are about to do business with your competitors so make it a great offer to lure them away) and hopefully you'll get some extra business.

Google doesn't like businesses owning multiple websites trying to target the same words. So if you're going to use this method:

- Register the domain with another domain register
- Use different registration details
- Use a different webhost
- Set up another Adwords account that doesn't matter if it gets blocked.

The website will need lots of content – but you can focus all of that content on why your spa is so good and create an amazing offer to pull them away from your competitors.

Use different details for everything: billing card, address, email. You don't want the two accounts to be able to be linked together. Host them on another website and register the domain away from GoDaddy.

You don't really want Google or the other search engines linking the two accounts together. If you are caught often at first they'll tell you not to do it again but in some cases they could block it straight away (and possibly penalize your current website – which is bad news). But having said that it can be a very powerful method to get extra customers. So use at your own risk!

That's why you want to use as many different details as you can, so it can't be connected to you.

Bonus TIP – Once a customer has entered their email address do not just take them back to your home page.

Take them to a specially created page that says something along the lines of "We are just about to email your 'free gift' that should be with you in about 10 minutes, while you're waiting please read / watch this".

People who have just taken some form of action and have shown commitment are much more likely to book now than they are 2 weeks later.

So create a page that gives them some amazing offer that they would be crazy to refuse and try and create some sense of urgency that they need to book now. Limited quantities, expires soon, etc.

You could have an offer that if they book now they can have a free return session in 'August' (or a quiet time) or buy now and they can bring a friend free for 'x' treatment (great for referrals) or get a free 15 minute extra treatment.

Think of something you can offer to try and get a booking there and then. Give them the best offer you can, something amazing.

Recently I heard about a company selling $50 vouchers for just $20. It was a great offer that a lot of people took up. They had raised their prices before to allow for the discount!

Plus people have that 'perceived value' the higher the price the better the quality.

Take Emails To The Next Level with Autoresponders

Autoresponders are a fantastic method that allow you to easily keep in touch with your customers and potential customers automatically without you having to do anything. Set up correctly autoresponders are one of my favourite methods of getting repeat business.

You know you need to keep in contact with your customers especially to drive repeat business. But doing mailshots can get quite expensive, especially if you want to send thousands.

Not only do you need to pay for the artwork to get set up, you've got the printing and distribution costs. Plus what if there is a mistake?

What about a customer who contacts you and asks for your details? Wouldn't you like to be able to send them everything immediately? But then also automatically follow up a few days later asking if they received it ok and if they had any questions?

Just a simple follow up can turn a browser into a buyer. If they don't buy then, what about contacting them a week or so later with an offer?

But hey I know you're busy, you've got other things to do, right?

Would you like the secret I use to drive repeat sales?

Well using Autoresponders allow you to set all this up in just a few simple steps.

Firstly it's important you understand what Autoresponders are.

They are basically a piece of software that allows you to reply automatically to customers who enquire by email.

Simply put if someone emails, you can set your email to send a reply automatically depending on what words are used in the email they sent or what email address they used.

Example - A customer emails returns@companyname.com – You could have an autoresponder that replies to any email it receives at returns@companyname.com to reply with full details on how to return a product and if they need any further information then contact (another email address). This email would be sent straight away. It doesn't matter if it's 2am on Sunday morning. The customer would receive an immediate reply.

Or you could simply have an email that replies to everything that says 'thank you for your email we'll be in contact ASAP....'

You can also set them so if it spots certain words in the customers email it will send a set reply. So if the customer writes "..... gift vouchers...." in their email, you can have it set so once it sees the word 'gift voucher' it automatically replies with your email giving them all the details they need on your gift vouchers.

Just a note that if you use lots of keywords and different autoresponder messages, it will often take the first keyword it spots in the email and use that as the reply.

These are fairly easy to set up and since all email accounts are different I would suggest you contact your email host (generally whoever you host your website through) and there will be some instructions in their FAQ pages. Just search for 'autoresponders'

Want to see where the real 'magic' happens?

There are some software services on the web that let you use autoresponders in far more creative ways and really make them very, very powerful. They are such a good way to communicate with your customers and go far beyond a simple automatic reply to an email.

Imagine being able to write a series of emails all at once telling your customers all about your spa and the services / products it offers and asking them to try it. Then if after that sequence of emails the customer hasn't booked you can offer them a special voucher that ONLY goes to those customers (not those who booked from your original emails and paid full price for your service) and you can automatically keep following up until they

45

either ask to be removed from your mailing list or become a customer.

Don't be afraid…

Especially with this set of 'pre-customers' don't be afraid of over emailing. Now I don't mean send 2 emails a day for a month. But there is nothing wrong in sending 5 or 6 emails within a 2-week period. Because often that is when the prospect is most interested in your service.

After that, slow the sequence down to perhaps just one email per week.

If a potential customer contacts a spa chances are they are looking to book either then or within a few days or at the very least are a strong possible customer lead.

So make sure you follow up with these potential customers and get your name in front of them for when they are ready to buy. So have 5 or 6 emails ready to go straight away.

After that time and they haven't purchased follow up with them every 1 or 2 weeks. You want to keep your name in their mind.

Now you DON'T want to keep emailing them the same email every week. It's boring and they'll either delete it or unsubscribe and you won't have any more chances to make that sale.

Useful TIP - One thing that is worth remembering, it's worth putting in place an autoresponder about 51 weeks after the initial contact from the customer saying something along the lines of "This time last year I don't know if you wanted to treat yourself or were looking for a gift, but I thought I'd drop you a quick

46

email and let you know about....(new services) and we've put together a very special offer...." You get the idea.

If they were buying a spa treatment as a gift, it's a useful reminder. Even if they didn't purchase last year they might this time. It doesn't take any effort on your part apart from writing one email; the autoresponder service will do the rest!

But generally your follow up emails should be a combination of useful information and offers. I usually go for two content followed by one promo.

Here's what to include in those autoresponder emails

Not sure what to write about? Ask your customers what they want to know more about. This is probably your best resource. Give customers the information they want to know about. You can look at books on spas to find out what topics are covered.

Are there any new techniques? You want to make your email something people want to read. It should be designed to position you as the expert in your field, the 'go to' people.

Include GREAT CONTENT that people want to read, share and tell their friends about.

- 9 Great ways to have a better message
- What you MUST know about spa treatments
- Can these oils relax you better than...
- Why having a spa could save your life...

Just make the subject line interesting enough that make people want to open your email. Then give them enough good content to make them read the email.

47

Do it once!

Now here's the magic: ALL these 'pre-customer' emails need to be written only once. Yes that's right, you do the work once load it into the software and for years to come it can automatically follow up your customers leaving you free to do the more fun things in your business.

But here's the bit I really like – using autoresponders for your current customers. When a customer orders you can take them off your 'pre-customers' and transfer them across to your 'customers' list.

After all you don't really want 'customers' receiving certain offers that you are using just to tempt that first booking, do you?

So once they have become a customer you want a slightly different approach in following them up.

Here's Your First Customer Follow Up Email

Your first email should be along the lines of 'thank you for your booking'.

- Here's what you'll need to bring, this is what to expect, here's how to find us, any questions....

Make it friendly and welcoming. Treat them as a valued customer, not just a booking. Making your customer feels special and creating the right first impression is vital so spend time making sure this is right.

You could even get a copywriter on Elance.com to write or polish up your emails to help them sell better. Writing high converting emails is a talent in itself.

Your Second Customer Email

Then after the booking, have a follow up email that says something along the lines of

-   "Thank you so much for coming to see us, it was great to see you and we really hope you enjoyed it....

    As you know we are a new family business who really care about our customers and want to try and let others know about our service. We would really appreciate it if you could leave a positive review at (review websites) any questions please get in contact...."

3rd **Email**

You can always follow up (automatically of course) a week later saying something like:

-   "Thank you for coming to see us... I've been so busy I haven't had chance to check if you were able to leave us a positive review. If you were thank you so much, if not is there any chance you could do it today please at.... It would really help at lot."

Getting those important customer reviews will be very important in gaining new business so you want to do everything possible to encourage it. Be sure to read the chapters on 'customer reviews'.

Then you'll want to keep in contact every 1 - 3 weeks or so. Again use a mixture of content and offers. If you have great content do it regularly. If you struggle for content only email once or twice a month. It's better your emails are read than simply binned or marked as spam!

These people are the easiest people you can sell to. You have already proved your service and they have trusted you. So treat them as special customers and try and make offers they can't refuse.

You should also contact these customers and ask them to refer you to their friends. They are a great source of new leads.

Read the Facebook marketing chapter because your customers email address can also be used to great effect when you are advertising on Facebook. You can do some very clever stuff. Almost certainly none of competitors know about this method.

I hope you start to see the power of these tips. When you fully understand and start to think of your own ways you'll discover how amazing this can be.

Someone contacts you just once and you can keep in contact with that person for years automatically offering your services. You could never do that using direct mail or Yellow Pages ads. This is really powerful.

Need extra business during quiet times?

Also imagine you normally have a quiet spell in the middle of August because everyone is away on holiday.

You can easily send out a newsletter to either your prospects or customers and come up with a great reason for doing a super offer…

- "Just to let you know that since everyone is away on holiday for the next couple of weeks we have a few rare late availability sessions. Since I still need to pay our staff I would rather we took some bookings. So I have decided to do our 'best offer of the year' if you book….." you get the idea.

You can use these to help get bookings for when you are normally quiet. It's also useful to give a reason for your offer as it becomes more genuine.

In the example above the customer can see why you are giving a discount. It's a quiet time of year yet you still have bills to pay so you want to fill some late availability. That way they won't expect discounts all the time, which is not what you want.

So whom do you use for your autoresponder?

There are loads of good solutions out there. But the company I have used for years is

Aweber.com

Now in all honesty I don't know how they compare on cost. They are probably about average. But I have found them faultless.

Their service is great and the software is easy to use even for the novice. I personally would rather pay more for them and use a quality product.

Aweber (you can sign up for just $1)

Plus you can start to do really clever stuff with Aweber.

For example you can personalise each email so you include your customer's name. It makes it far more personalised and there's a higher chance the email will be opened.

If you only want to send them an email on a Tuesday morning you can.

In your sequence of emails you can say watch out for a special email from me in 5 days (and it can then automatically insert the date 5 days from then). You just need to think of some great ways to use it.

If you want to see exactly how to set up the autoresponder messages in Aweber you can get the free video from SpaBusinessMarketing.com.

53

Blow Your Customers Away With a Special Spa Marketing
Product Trip Wire

What can YOU do or offer that your competitors will think
you're crazy to be doing? What would get your customers
queuing around the block?

Can you blow your competition out of the water by giving
customers no option but to pick you to do business with?

Create a product so good and then give it away at a fantastic
price.

You might also hear this referred to as the

Visit www.SpaBusinessMarketing.com for MORE expert advice

Irresistible Spa Marketing Offer

Let me give you a few examples...

1 - I've heard of a guy on Ebay who has a massive guitar shop in America. He sells anything and everything for guitarists. He wants to find and target guitar owners. The more of these he can locate cheaply the greater the chance he has to sell them stuff, especially new guitars where I imagine he makes his money.

So what did he come up with as his 'Product Trip Wire / Irresistible Offer'? Simple! What do most guitarists use? A guitar pick.

He buys thousands of them from China (and if he's got any sense he'll put his website address on them) but more importantly he sells them at cost.

How can anyone compete against him when he is buying in bulk from China and selling at cost? There is simply no profit in it for anyone. So if you are after a guitar pick from whom do you buy? Him - If you need a guitar pick what do you own? A guitar, you're his 100% perfect customer.

He has built up a massive database of guitar owners who have already purchased from him (and established some form of trust / relationship - remember it is easier to sell again to a current customer than it is to get a new one). So he can easily target them with great offers to sell his more profitable items.

Plus effectively it's not costing him anything to acquire these customers. No pay per click stuff, no crazy newspaper ads. Just guitar picks sold at cost.

2 - I heard of another guy who wanted to break into the 'candle making supply' business. What do all candle makers need? Wicks - you can't make a candle without a wick.

So what was his 'Product Trip Wire / Irresistible Offer'?

Again he simply found a supplier and imported candle wicks. I believe in this case he actually sold them below cost because he knew he would sell more than anyone and the money was in the back end; the lifetime customer value.

How can anyone compete against him? Anyone else selling candle stuff would just think he's crazy and will probably soon go out of business. But if you need a candle wick who do you choose?

But again he built up a huge database of candle makers to whom he could then simply offer more candle supply materials. He could then sell them wax, containers, etc.

It's as simple as that –

What can you offer that will set you apart?

It becomes harder on a single purchase item where the lifetime value of the customer is limited. Here you need to make your product irresistible.

I knew a guy who sold inflatable kayaks. There really isn't much of a backend business here. So he made his guarantee unique. He said the customer had a "90 day try it at home money back guarantee... take it on the water, use it, love it and if you don't totally enjoy it we'll give you your money back."

Yes the customers in theory could take it on a 2-week holiday, enjoy it for the summer and return it for their money back.

Do you know how many customers took him up on that offer? One - that's all. But his competition never copied him. So in the customer's mind who has more trust in their product? Where would you buy?

But in the Spa business you need valuable repeat customers.

I believe every business can come up with a product trip wire. You just need to have a really good think about how you can monetize the back end or do something the competition can't or is unwilling to do.

Could you offer a free 15-minute massage? Go around to local businesses and leave leaflets with them about your offer.

Once the customer has enjoyed the offer you simply ask

58

- "Did you enjoy that?" Customer "Yes"
  You reply "Great would you like another?" Customer (perhaps thinking it might be free again) "Yes"
  You "Great we've got a special offer on at the moment just to welcome new clients. You can get (give them an amazing offer) .... normally x for just y - Does that sound good?"
  Customer "Yes" - You "Great when would you like to schedule your appointment?"

If nothing else you'll collect their details so you can follow them up with other offers and all it cost you was 15 minutes of your time.

It often takes guts to create a product trip wire. But if you get it right it can work wonders in helping you to gather more customers.

What about buying a load of the oils you use and packaging them up with your own label on. Make them look fantastic (you could easily spend more on the packaging than the oils themselves but the impression is really important). If you buy a lot you should be able to great a price.

If not, find a manufacturer (you want a manufacturer so you get the lowest possible price) who can give you a great deal. You could Google 'massage oils wholesale', 'massage oil manufacturers'

Then go into shops around your area and offer these bottles to them at the same price you pay. That should give them a fantastic profit margin so they should be keen, especially if you offered it on sale or return (if it doesn't sell they can return the unsold bottles).

Normally that shop couldn't buy anywhere near the manufacturer's cost since it normally goes through suppliers, wholesalers, agents etc. who all mark it up.

Now your customer can sell a bottle for say $10 that only cost them $1.50; so they are happy.

Because you were smart you put all your contact details and a fantastic offer on the back of the bottle.

USEFUL TIP - If you use a different website domain you'll even be able to track exactly how successful this promotion is.

You then have all these great little bottles in retailers in your target area providing you great highly targeted advertising and positioning you as the dominant expert in your area.

Could you even get a miniature bottle and give it to local hoteliers in your area to give to their customers – with of course a great offer for your spa?

Think where your customers are locally – gyms? What offer can you create for the gym owner that gives them and their customers a great deal? Could you offer an evening for their gym members at a reduced rate?

Retailers are happy since they have great product margins, customers get the oils they wanted and you get the chance to get more customers. It's like companies who advertise on the back of cereal packets. They do it because it works. You can use the same idea.

When you know your numbers you can even take this a step further. If you know that every customer is worth $100 profit over 2 years you could offer that owner a nice incentive to send you customers. You could pay them $20 for every customer referral they give you.

You could create a leaflet that has a great offer on. Give it to local shops and explain to them that each set of leaflets is unique to them. You could use a special voucher code for each location that offers the leaflets.

Then when a customer books using that voucher code you know it was X store that referred the customer. You can then reward that store owner with a bonus.

To make your business really successful you need to make more money per customer than you spend to acquire them and more than your competitors.

That allows you to spend more money to acquire each customer. So if a competitor went into that shop and in the unlikely event they tried to copy your method of selling the bottles you could go back to the retailer and improve your offer. Give the retailer more money to stop the competitor if you have to.

Often on the front end you just want to break even. Your real profit comes by turning that customer into a repeat customer and by them referring others.

Would You Like More Customers Than You Can Handle? The
Secret – Referrals and Being Found Locally

Now it's no good having the greatest website in the world if no
one knows it even exists. You need to get targeted visitors to
your website in order to have any chance of making a sale to
them.

The better you do this part the better the chance you have of
making good profits. More visitors should mean more customers
and bigger profits.

Now if you do this bit right you can get regular highly targeted
customers every week just looking to do business with a spa
centre like yours. These are people who have specially gone on to
a website to search for what you are offering.

You can't get a better customer target!

It's really important you do this correctly and spend time doing
it. You can get these customers free once you've done the work in
setting this up.

Free customers give you better profits since you haven't had to spend any advertising money to acquire them. So follow this method.

If done properly and done well you may not even need many of the other forms of advertising. You can stick with these free customers that the likes of Google and Yahoo can provide you with daily.

Years ago you would have probably searched the phone book to find a local business. Nowadays almost everyone just searches the web.

Important - So that is where your spa needs to be found and it needs to be listed higher up in the search engines than your competitors so people click on your site first.

The revolution in local search is happening now and now is the time to establish your presence.

At the moment the competition are only just starting to understand the power of this but over the next few years the competition will catch on.

By then you want to be far in front with loads of happy customer reviews and ratings. It starts to make it harder for the competition to compete with you.

Quick Example

Simply put if you saw 2 spa's in Google, one was your Spa with 55 happy glowing customer reviews and the other had 3, which would you choose?

You'd probably choose you. Most people will follow the crowd. Therefore you need to get established now and start with local

63

marketing on the search engines. It is very effective. The better the reviews and the more you have the better your chances are of acquiring the customers.

So start to follow the step-by-step strategies I'm about to reveal. It's a big chapter but worth your time if you want to be the #1 Spa in your area on Google. Using these methods you can achieve this.

So what is local search?

It's just like the phone book but in much greater detail. Go ahead and test it out. Search Google for a local service like 'Spa and your area'. Now Google keep altering how they display these but you'll see something like

I searched for 'Spa Surrey' so you can see that Google returned a map. All the dots indicate a spa and the 'Letter icons' represent

the results it listed above (A-F) you can already see that some of these places have reviews.

I already know that if I was a searcher I'd be unlikely to click on 'Champneys' as their reviews look the worst. If I was them I would now need to concentrate hard on getting more positive reviews urgently. At the moment it's almost certainly costing them lost sales. You don't want that to happen to you!

Don't worry you will get the odd bad review but I'll show you how to get hoards of raving fans so that it really won't matter (the odd bad review also makes you look genuine) People know that you can't please everyone all the time.

Also in the image above you can see some paid ads in the right column.

But 'Local Search' can put your business in front of people looking for your service so you need to do it. It simply connects the online world with the offline world. Plus it's happening more and more with mobile search via smartphones.

You need to be on:

Google

Yahoo / Bing

Yelp

Apple Maps

The GOOD NEWS – You can beat the Big Boys

At the moment with local search you can outrank national brands because they find it very hard to compete on a local search with a national presence and with so many locations.

- Again this is your opportunity to get in and dominate this area.

Just a TIP right off - you'll want to use a local phone number rather than a free phone or geographic free number. Those other numbers are fine to use on your advertising but if Google can see a local number it helps them know your location really easily.

Correct Details?

You might already be listed in the search engines. They pull a lot of data from various business directories.

You want to make sure that your business name, address and phone number are all the same throughout any listings. If not you should start trying to change it. Remember use your local phone number rather than your Freephone (save that for your ads).

Get Google's Trust – It Will Help You

Google want to give current, accurate results to their customers. If they have data on you with different names, phone numbers, locations etc. they can get confused. That in turn gives you less trust with them and they'll rank someone else above you who they trust more!

So you want all your info to be the same.

Once you are correctly listed in Google you should start to appear in:

Google Maps

Google Places

Google Business Listings

Google Local

And more....

So How Do Google Determine Who They List First?

It's the same as when you search anything on Google. They go into their massive database of knowledge and quickly sift through it to try and give you the best possible results.

Their sifting of results (known as algorithm) is very complicated. It's thought they check over 500 bits of information before giving you the results.

That information is weighted in importance and changes over time. They never tell you the exact formula they use!

You'll even find you get different results depending on if you search using a PC or tablet or mobile and what you have searched for in the past.

Even how they display the results to you will change. They are constantly trying to improve them. That is why you need to help them as much as possible by giving them the best and correct information everywhere you are listed.

Google own the information and their computers decide how you rank. You can't contact them and tell them that you are better than x. Or that competitor x has terrible reviews and is still listed above you. It doesn't work like that. It might not be fair but that is life under the search engines.

You'll also find over time that Google change the guidelines they give and the way they rank sites. They will not tell you before, they just go ahead and do it!

They will give you guidelines but those are 'rough guides' at best so that spammers don't find ways of getting around the rules.

You can read more at

https://support.google.com/places/answer/107528?hl=en

and

https://support.google.com/places/

Behave Yourself – It 'Could' Cost You Your Business If You Don't!

Please DO NOT break the rules. It may work short term (or even for a few years) but when they find out, you could be removed from their index. In short your customer won't be able to find you. At worst it could put you out of business.

When signing up with Google use your business email e.g. clare@myspaname.com rather than a free email address. If multiple people are going to use the account use an email like customers@myspaname.com

You need to have a presence in the area you want listed and you need to be up and running. You can't get listed with 'coming soon'. You need the authority to list the place that you want listed.

Listing your Business Name

It must be exactly as people would see and use it off line. You are not allowed any strap lines or website addresses (unless they are part of your company name and listed elsewhere exactly the same).

Some companies have even changed their business name to include their keywords.

In the past having your keywords (terms that you wanted to be found under) in your business name helped you rank higher. The importance of this is thankfully going down (although I think it still does help).

Locations –

Again you must use your physical address. You can't hide behind PO Boxes and you can only have one listing for each location.

This address must match your other business listings to start giving you trust marks in Google's eyes.

If you are a mobile spa you need to click "Yes this business serves customers at their locations" under the 'Service Area & Location Settings'.

For more information on detailing your service you can visit

https://support.google.com/places/answer/177103?hl=en

You can choose a certain radius from your location or certain areas.

Website and Phone Numbers

They say "Provide a phone number that connects to your individual business location as directly as possible, and provide one website that represents your individual business location.

- Use a local phone number instead of a call centre number whenever possible.
- Do not provide phone numbers or URLs that redirect or "refer" users to landing pages or phone numbers other than those of the actual business."

So that means you can't (or you can but it will not help you) use mobile numbers or non geo graphic numbers. It maybe your number that you advertise but Google doesn't want that!

They probably do it because it's harder to pretend you are doing business in a certain area if you don't have a local number.

It helps stop national brands pretending they are local. So think of it as a positive way to try and help your spa get a few bonus trust marks.

When you enter your website use the website address that is actually hosted e.g. www.SpaPlaceName.com rather than the name that is merely pointing to that site. Again you'll get extra marks for having a website over those businesses that don't.

Choose Your Category

"Select at least one category from the list of available categories.

- Categories should depict what your business is (e.g. *Hospital*), not what it does (e.g. *Vaccinations*) or

70

products it sells (e.g. *Sony products* or *printer paper*). This information can be added in your description."

Pick the category that is the closet match to what you do.

Google are the experts in knowing what people want when they search. For example, if someone searches for 'dog limping' Google will know from its history that you might need a vet and may return results for a local vet. Or if you search for 'car breakdown' you may well see local garages.

You can select the categories that closest match your business. Don't go and pick categories that are not relevant just because you think more people will search for that topic!

Try and choose from the categories Google provide. It can hurt your listings if you start entering your own! As an example, don't go and enter 'Miami Spa'. That is not allowed.

So You Are Ready To Submit Your Business?

First thing you'll need is a free Google account. Try and use a trusted email address that has already been registered with Google rather than a new email account. Also make it a general account that everyone who needs access in your business can access.

If you use an individual email what happens if that person leaves?

https://accounts.google.com/SignUp

71

When you submit your listing to Google they will check and see if you are already listed. If they find a match they'll ask you if you want to claim the listing. You'll have 2 options:

- By phone
- By post

If you choose to do it by phone be sure you have access to the phone number listed. They'll call you and give you a code that you have to enter on the screen straight away.

This is great in that you can be verified straight away. If you have to do it by post Google will send you a card in the post with a unique number that you'll need to enter.

At the end of the day you want to give Google the best, most detailed and accurate information you can. They want to return the best results. By giving them great data it should help Google rank you higher than companies that don't provide such good trusted data (after all what you entered matches other listings you have on the web.)

When you enter your business description think of it as an 'elevator pitch' it MUST BE short and sweet. Around 200 characters is fine. Write a normal sentence. Don't start each word with Capitals! Don't stuff keywords in there, or repeat your area name.

Think of something that would compel you to click your listing over a competitor. Write something **persuasive**. I've heard that this description does not affect your ranking now. But again that could change at any time.

Use great photos as well – make your company stand out. But use photos of your business not some stock photo. It often helps if you can get a person in the photo. Use large, good quality images. If you don't, Google may well take images from your website that you don't want used!

You can also include video. With videos being so easy to record on your mobile go ahead and record something. Then give it to someone on Elance to turn into a professional production. It shouldn't cost much and will help you stand out from your competitors. Don't use quick easy video from your mobile without any editing or production. It will just make you look cheap!

You want to give Google ALL the information they ask for. For example when they ask for opening and closing times, provide them. Help Google every step of the way.

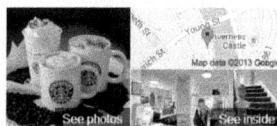

Visit www.SpaBusinessMarketing.com for MORE expert advice

You can see in the listing above (although the layout is likely to change) one way Google can present the results to you.

You can see the maps and photos.

TIP - Think how you could use photos to entice people to click on your listing. You'll want to use great interesting photos. Images of people can work really well and help draw the eye to get you noticed.

It also displays your address and contact details. Plus it tells you where the reviews are coming from. There are 5 from Google and you can get other reviews from Booking.com, TripAdvisor.com and others … where do you think you need to get your customers to leave rave reviews!!!!

When I compared that listing to others on the page. They were the only ones that had reviews and a complete profile!

Others may have had reviews but were missing certain photos etc.

You see how providing ALL the information can help get you a top listing.

TIP - You only really need to do a better job than the few competing sites in your area. Since most don't have a clue about internet marketing you are ready to gain customers.

Using Google Maps To Your Advantage

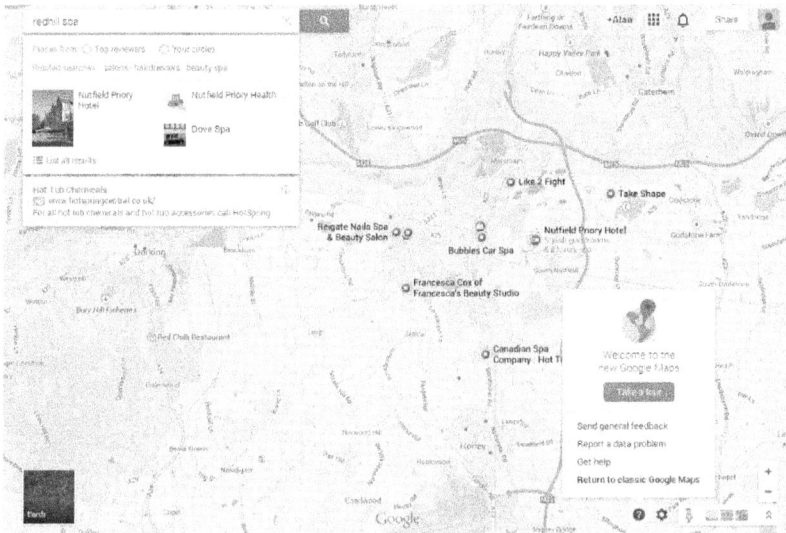

The way Google display businesses on maps has changed again. You can see the new version above (although expect more changes).

The option above clearly gives the user the ability to search by 'Reviews'. It is going to become more and more important to start generating positive reviews.

You can also filter by 'Your circles'. You'll want to get customers to +1 your site.

Plus an advert powered by Google's 'Adwords Express'.

If you click on a pin you'll see more detailed business information.

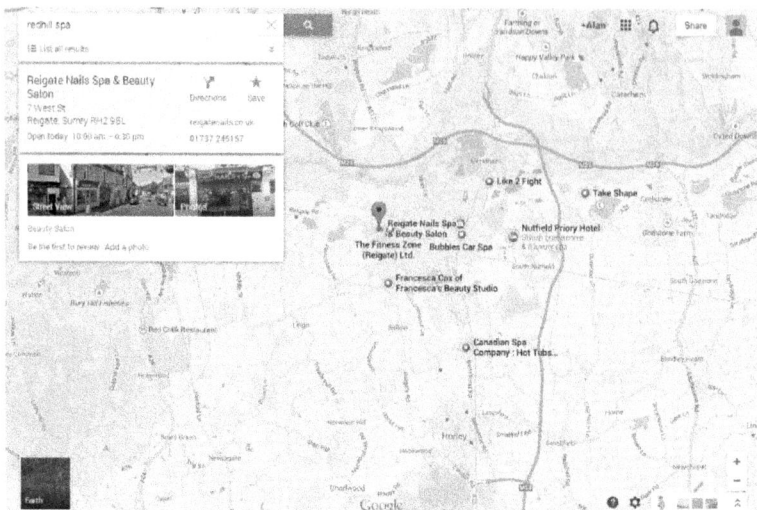

It looks like this business hasn't done much with their listing. Google has used the Street View images. So be sure to do the best job you can of providing compelling information.

Remember that customers may also start searching for you using their mobile, especially if they are walking to you. You'll want to make sure that your map pin is in exactly the right spot. You can alter that if you need to from within your Google account on street view. You need to use 'Fix incorrect marker location'.

Pretend you are a customer and check to ensure everything is appearing as it should. If not go into your listings and correct it. It may take a while before your changes filter through to what you see on screen.

You Need Facebook and NOW Google+

Google realised it had lost a lot of ground to Facebook. Google after all is a data company and wants as much information as it can about its users. Google+ is it's answer to Facebook and they are trying to push it as much as they can.

They want to push it so they can collect reviews and more social data. The idea is that if a friend of yours has used a certain spa Google will have that knowledge and is more likely to feature that result to you by saying 'Your friend x has visited....' You should also be able to see recommendations from your friends – trusted reviews!

In the future they'll almost certainly try and push other features (and probably try and push advertising). Either way since your customers will probably end up using it you need to create a free account if you don't already have a Google+ account at - https://plus.google.com/

Then from the 'Home' icon at the top left, from the dropdown click

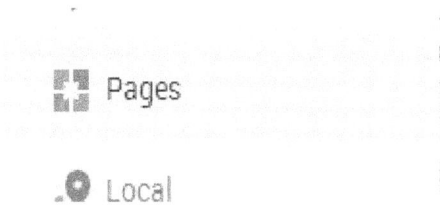

Pages

Local

'Pages'

Then 'Create a Page' (upper right).

Then select the local business or place.

Enter the name or address of your business if it appears in the dropdown. If it doesn't appear you'll be able to enter your business details.

Make sure these details are correct. You can then verify the details as you have before by phone or postcard.

Once you've signed up you'll be able to see stats about your page and the way people are interacting with it.

Go to https://support.google.com/plus/answer/3154791 for more information.

Yahoo Local Is Also Important!

Yahoo is still an important search engine and whilst most of your visitors will probably come from Google you still need to spend some time managing your Yahoo presence.

Their results look similar to Google's

reading spa | Search

Search ● the Web ○ only in UK ○ only in Ireland

Spa near Reading
uk.local.yahoo.com

1. Aquarius Pool Services
   (07970) 252512 - 68 Park View Drive North, RG10 9QY Reading
   Get Directions

2. Hotspring World Reading
   (0118) 986 3302 - 656 Reading Road Garden Centre House,
   RG41 5HG Wokingham
   Get Directions

3. Esprit Fitness & Spa
   (0118) 944 4221 - Eskdale Road, RG41 5TS Wokingham
   Get Directions

More Results...

You can get a free local listing on Yahoo at

http://smallbusiness.yahoo.com/local-listings/basic-listing/

One thing to remember with Yahoo Local is the importance of 'Good Reviews'. They really value them and you can get good rankings if you can collect some good reviews.

Again make sure all the information you give is accurate and there are no errors. Any reviewer should be able to confirm the information you provide is the same as on your website.

You'll notice that Yahoo Local also offer 2 premium products:

http://smallbusiness.yahoo.com/local-listings/compare-plans/

Yahoo Localworks - $29.99 monthly. Personally I don't think the extra cost is worth it. Billed over the year you are charged almost $360. For that they'll enter you into 40 directories!

To be honest you'll probably find you are listed in some of these directories anyway. Or go via Elance and get someone to do it for

79

you for a one off fee (someone might do it in total for $100). Otherwise in 10 years it may have cost you $3,600.

However, you may find the 'Local Enhanced' version worth the $9.99 monthly. You can include photos, a long business description and 2 links to your site.

Think of it like the 'larger yellow pages ad'; the larger ad gives you extra trust! You also get more control over how your results appear and of course a trusted link from Yahoo!

Bing Places (Microsoft)
https://www.bingplaces.com/

This is a very similar process to Yahoo and Google. However if you click 'Verify by phone' at the end of the process they will call you straight away. If you don't answer the phone it can be a real pain to get verified!

So either make sure you can answer the phone number you entered or simply verify by post. It takes longer but can save a huge amount of problems.

Again follow their straight forward step-by-step process.

Spend a few minutes a month doing this...

As with all your local accounts login every month or two and ensure all the details are correct, update a description, maybe change a photo. It helps the search engines to know that you are actively checking your listings and you're still in business.

All things being equal who do you think they would prefer to list – an account that was created 3 years ago and had no updates or an account created 2 years ago that has had a few regular updates?

- *You don't have to do a huge amount. Just do more than your competition and do it better!*

To help your business feature well I would also suggest having your address in the footer of your website (that is the bit at the bottom of the website that appears on all your pages and also has a link to your terms and conditions). It just reinforces your location to the search engines.

You may also wish to list your business in other local directories.

Important – Make sure the information you enter into ALL these directories is the SAME as you entered into the big 3 directories. Otherwise you might end up doing more harm than good. The search engines want consistence results.

YellowPages.com

Yp.aol.com

Local.com

Superpages.com

TIP - There may also be other industry specific pages. The best thing to do is search Google and Yahoo for your keywords e.g.

Reading Spa

And see if any directory results are returned in the main listings (not local listings). If so make sure you get listed in them.

Visit the site and somewhere there should be an 'add business' link. If you can't see it contact them.

81

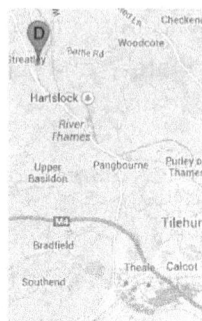

Map for **reading spa**

You would be wise to get listed in Wahanda and TripAdvisor since Google is returning results from these directories for the phrase 'Reading Spa'.

The more chances you have for a customer to find you, the better your chances are of making a sale.

Don't just search the first page, go through the first 3 or 4 pages. Again they all count as a trusted link to your website which will help you overall.

If you get enough trusted links you'll feature in the main results by yourself, which is what you want.

Bonus TIP –

Also search for 'local business directory' this should display the top local directories for your area. Again try and get listed in these.

You don't want listings in thousands of directories. You are fair better off with 20 trusted listings than 1000 computer auto submitted listings.

Important - Think trust and quality every time and you will not go too far wrong. If it looks like a cheap and nasty site don't add your details. Only submit to useful quality sites.

When you are getting listed in the Yellow Pages and the various local directories, personally I would just select the 'free' option.

Generally they don't get enough traffic to make paid ads worth it. But just by having a free ad, it should be enough for the search engines to find you.

Don't

If you purchase any ads make sure they DO NOT give you a location free number (or tracking phone number). Otherwise you'll have 2 numbers across the web and the search engines don't know what to trust – your rankings could suffer!

A lot of local marketing companies may offer you this so results can be tracked. It may be good for them but not for you. Your free listings may be harmed and you'll end up paying more for ads than you otherwise might!

Make The Most Of Apple –

With so many people using iPads and iPhones you also need to be featured on Apple Map searches.

At the moment it is thought Apple get their data from Localeze, Acxiom, Yelp and InfoGroup (again make sure your details are correct).

83

Because it's a newer system, it's not so complex and you stand a better chance of getting your business listed.

To get listed you need to use Apple Maps

1) Open the Apple Maps apps
2) Search for your business name
3) Select the page fold in the bottom right
4) Select <u>Report a Problem</u>
5) Select <u>Location is missing</u>, then <u>Next</u>
6) Position the pin to the correct location, then <u>Next</u>
7) Enter your business details, **don't forget to enter the business name!**
8) Make sure you select a category
9) Finally, select <u>Send</u>

How important is a Yelp Listing?

In short – Very!

If you get listed well in Yelp you'll probably get a good listing on Apple Maps and Bing! Plus Yelp say their app is on 8 million smartphones, so they account for a lot of searches in their own right.

To get a good listing on Yelp you need 'reviews' - the more good ones the better. I talk elsewhere about how to encourage good reviews but they are becoming increasingly important.

One thing to remember is that your information can appear in Yelp a few times because they do not require any verification process. That can lead to problems for you both on Yelp and local searches on other engines.

You need to ensure all your details are correct, look out for differences in address, phone numbers, etc. You only want 1 listing so that all your reviews are together on one page and so that search engines see 100% correct details about your business.

If you find any wrong information you can email Yelp and they should correct it for you. It is worth monitoring these results.

Once you have 'unlocked' your listing you can manage the listing so you can update hours and offers, etc.

Yelp Reviews....

These are really important but are weighted differently. One review can count much more than another person's review.

To stop companies trying to spam the system Yelp rewards reviewers who are active and leave lots of reviews rather than the person who just leaves one review and never returns.

Be warned Yelp do not want you to pay / encourage positive reviews. In fact let me put that another way, if they catch you incentivizing reviews in any way they can ban you from the directory – that could be a LOT of lost business. They want honest feedback. But as a business, of course you want the most active Yelp reviewers to give you a great review since it will help you massively!

You decide what route you want to take – but I personally would stay the right side of the line.

Note - You can encourage reviews but do not incentivize!

Would You Like To Know Where Your Customers Found You?
– Answer Google Analytics

Years ago John Wanamaker said, "Half my advertising is wasted, I just don't know which half." Today thankfully you don't have to waste money on unprofitable ads. Why? Because you can track almost everything you do and what advertising works best for you.

This is another secret that can put you miles in front of your competitors

If you see their ads everywhere without some form of tracking you can take a good guess that they are wasting money.

If you track everything and know what generates you customers, you can put more investment behind those methods. You can potentially pay more than your competitors because you know what works and they don't!

At the end of the day you want to focus your activities where it generates the most business for you. How do you know if one activity you do is responsible for 90% of your business. You don't unless you can track your results.

That's where Google Analytics comes in. It's a free tool that Google provide and it can help you track your results and discover what's working. You can then change your other approaches and test different things without destroying what is working for you.

The great thing is you can track where your visitors came from. So you are targeting a larger area and can see if most of your visitors came from certain locations.

If you are using different landing pages for various offers you can see which pages result in the most conversions.

Top TIP - You could produce leaflets that have offer x on and send them to yourwebsite.com/offerX and another set of leaflets could send them to yourwebsite.com/offerY – that way you can see if offer x or y resulted in more traffic. You then know what offer is working best for you.

Or if you want people to call in, ask them to mention Offer X or Offer Y and keep track.

Do more of what works. Come up with new offers and ideas and test those against your best advertising.

Once you have a Google account you can login to 'Google Analytics' and simply follow their instructions on how to set up a new site.

www.google.com/analytics/

If you get stuck either search for 'Google Analytics' and look at the results or go to YouTube and search for 'install Google Analytics'. Otherwise it would take up so many pages in this book there would be no room for other great content!

Basically you enter your website details and they'll give you a few lines of code. Copy and paste that code and put it at the bottom of all your website pages. It won't be visible to customers, but it will track what your customers do.

If you start selling services directly on your website (which I would encourage) you can track your conversion rate and then try and work out how to improve it.

You'll get data on your website either as a whole or page by page. You'll start to learn how long your visitors stay, what pages they visit, and what pages they exit from. If you start looking at the stats you can work out how to improve.

There are lots of good books on Analytics if you want to go into it deep. But really you just need an understanding of:

- How many visitors your website is getting
- Where they are coming from
- What are they doing on your site

What to do with the data?

It doesn't need to be any more complicated than that. If you know how many visitors you are getting but the phone isn't ringing you'll know your offer is wrong.

When you know where your visitors are coming from, you can work out what your best source of visitors is, try to improve it, and do more of what is generating customers.

If people are coming to your site and leaving straight away you know the design / content is a problem (bounce rate).

Again remember your competitors probably never look at any of this stuff. If you get your site working like a well-oiled sales machine it can be a great customer generator. You just need to make sure it works.

Don't forget to also check the various local dashboards offered by Google, Yahoo and Bing.

So How Do You Rank Well Locally?

Make sure ALL the listings of your company online use the:

- Same company name
- Same address
- Same phone number

There should be no variations (especially different phone numbers so you can track calls) don't do it - it can harm your local search results.

You also need a mobile friendly / responsive website that uses your keywords and phrases throughout (no spam, Google just needs to know the topic) and have the same contact details as listed elsewhere.

Competition is tough for the top listings and only going to get tougher. So take time and do it right so you beat the competition.

So why do you need to beat your competitors online?

I don't have stats for local searches but when you consider the top listing in Google results gets around 30 - 35% of all the page clicks – that's a massive amount of potential customers.

NO. 2 gets 15 – 20%, No. 3 nearer 10%, No. 4 between 5 – 10%. By position 10 it's 1 – 5% and on the second page not much!

Understand this point...

Getting the top listing is vitally important even for supposedly 'offline businesses' – because even these businesses are being found online and you NEED to be discovered ahead of your competitors so you have the chance to convert them into a customer before your competitors do.

TIP / Remember – once they are on your website do everything you can to capture their contact details so you can follow up with them.

Next offer them a great low cost offer to make that first transaction. If that first purchase can be an impulse buy e.g. under $20 even better. You stand to get far more customers. That customer has just become far more valuable to you and your business.

Create a product that you can then upsell to them by offering value and service. For example, buy 4 spa sessions for the price of 2, or buy 2 spa sessions and receive x, y, and z free.

After you have delivered, tempt them to come back again and again.

It all came from positioning your spa ahead of your competitors and following the formula.

So if you want to grow your spa business you need to do this correctly and well. It is very important.

As I said before all you really need to do is a better job than your local competitors (although doing the best job you can at the start can help protect and strengthen your business from any competitors that may come in the future). Start building solid results and a good reputation now. It makes it harder for them to overtake you.

Do Your Homework!

Understand your competitors. Take a look at what makes their listings and website successful

1 – Take a look at their website. How do they feature their location and main keywords? For example, is 'Reading Spa' a headline on the homepage like "The most relaxing spa in Reading"? That would be preferable to "Enjoy the most relaxing experience you'll ever have" (no keywords in that second phrase).

Look at their page names and how they link together, e.g. a link on their home page that reads, "Read our Spa Reviews" is better than "Read our Reviews" and "How to find us in Reading" is better than "How to Find Us".

When you create new pages
Websitename.com/spareviews.htm is better than
websitename.com/reviews.htm
And
Websitename.com/readingspa.htm is better than
websitename.com/howtofindus.htm

(But don't overdo it – use different keywords for each page. Don't call each page ReadingSpaReviews, ReadingSpaContactUs, ReadingSpaHowToFindUs – mix it up e.g. SpaReviews, ContactUs, FindUsInReading, etc.

2- Here's a great TIP. Search engines love trust. I've already mentioned how you want your information the same on all the sites to help build trust.

If you had Microsoft.com, Apple.com, BBC.co.uk, Sky.com all link to your new Spa business you'd be No. 1 in Google for almost any term you choose! Why? Because Google trusts those sites only to link to other good resources.

It makes Google's job easier. It knows that if lots of 'trusted sites' link to you, you must be good! However if no one links to you it wonders why. Equally, if all it finds is thousands of spammy websites linking to you – guess what it thinks?

So how can you tell what sites link to your competitors? Simple! Get a month's subscription to

www.SEOMajestic.com

www.Ahrefs.com

(Join for the first month and then cancel, you probably will not need more than that.)

You can enter your competitor's website into their search box and it will tell you what other websites link to them. Don't just do it for one competitor do it for ALL the competitors you can find.

You can also include competitors outside your direct area. Then ignore the local links they have. But you might find a link from a national directory that is trusted, or a press article where you may be able to get a link in the future.

This process allows you to find the most trusted sites and links. Next you'll want to create a list. Guess what? – You then need to go and try and get a link from all the top rated sites that link to your competitors.

Links from these sites are gold dust and can help give you a number 1 ranking. You could offer to write an article / content for them. Offer their members a special offer or free gift, or even pay for a link.

The more trusted the link to a competitor's website, the more you need to focus on achieving a link to your own website.

If you owned that site what would want to make you link to your current site? What's in it for them? What can improve their site? Often links from sites like this can take a few weeks (or longer) to achieve. Follow up and provide help, advice, and build a relationship.

One good way would be to contact them and provide something of service without even asking for a link. Later you could say that you linked to them and would they consider linking to you.

Also remember to contact and link to other quality local businesses. They can help pass on customers and build up your 'local' profile.

3 – How many Google+ and other reviews do they have? On sites like Google they seem to be putting less emphasis on reviews than sites like Yelp. But either way you want as many positive reviews as you can get.

People are far more likely to post negative reviews (people like moaning!) than positive ones. So you need to encourage those positive reviews as much as you can.

To beat your competitors - Summary

- Make sure you have claimed your listing in Google, Yahoo, Bing and Yelp and that all your details are 100% correct and the same on each site and keep them updated.

- Make sure you're listed in various business directories, both local and those that relate to your business. Again trusted quality resources. Don't use a bulk directory submitter.

- Try and get local press mentions and local people talking about you. Can you do something fun that makes people talk? Giving to local charities in exchange for a link on their website? Anything that gets people talking and writing about you.

- Having keywords in your business name will help. If your business is called "Readings Relaxing Spa" it will help more than "Sally's Spa" but you cannot just go entering keywords into your company name on your various listings if your business is not registered as that name. It could cause your listing to be removed.

- Where are you based? If your spa is based in the centre of your town / city it will be much better than if you are a few miles away.

  If someone searches 'Reading Spa' the search engine wants to return results as close to the middle of the town as possible. If you are 10 miles outside it will make it harder for you to be listed! That being said search engines are getting smarter and know that people will travel for various services like spas so they are getting better at including more locations. However, being centrally located will help.

Other sites linking to you with your area and keyword will also help a lot (BUT just make sure they don't all link the same way, only a fraction should link this way – a BIG warning sign to search engines. Try and get the most important links using them).

- Reviews, I've said it before, you really want to try and create hoards of screaming fans that want to tell the world about how wonderful you are!

 In short the more positive reviews you receive the better it will be. Particularly if they are from trusted reviewers (e.g. people who have already reviewed lots of other services) and on trusted sites like Yelp and Trip Advisor.

People like doing business with companies that have lots of positive reviews. If you saw 2 spas and one had 25 four and five-star reviews and the other had only three, you are more likely to click the one with more reviews.
-
- Sometimes you can even sort sites based on reviews. You want more positive ones than your competitors and do what you can to achieve that. It gets harder the longer you wait. So start now!

- Use great photos and videos to make your listing stand out from everyone else's.

- Obtain links from local trusted sources: your Chambers of Commerce, local press and businesses. Can you get links from sites that 'relate' to your spa? Hair salons for example? Quality over quantity every time.

- Your domain. When you registered your domain did you use your business address? If not, go and alter your domain record. Go back to the place where you registered it and change it. If you already used your business address then that's great, but make sure the information is publically visible and you didn't put any privacy policies in place (you can often opt out). If you did opt out contact your domain register and opt back in. You can check by looking at WhoIs.net – do you see your details?

- On your website have your full address (no abbreviations) listed at the bottom of every page. Tell your web developer you want it marked for Scheme.org Include your phone number with area code. If you have a toll / free number you can use both but make sure you include your normal landline.

- Make sure you list your opening and closing times and that they are the same as you have listed elsewhere on the web.

- Website page names. Include your area and keywords in lots of your page names. Again it helps back up the search engine knowledge of where you are based.

- When you use images on your website use the 'alt' tag. Again your web developer will know. But when you put your mouse over the image it should describe the image used.

- Use H1 tag in your headline for your most important location and keyword. You can only use 1 set of H1 tags per page. Use a good Meta description. Often this is the description the search engines will display to visitors.

  This description is good as it encourages the user to click on the listing "ultimate in relaxation.... Fully restored" is much better than "A Spa started by me and my husband in 1980...." Which listing would you click?

- The text elsewhere on the page should also be all about your spa but don't go putting text like "we have the best spa in reading, reading spa, if you need a spa in reading etc..." on your page. Just use natural language. Use your keywords but don't over do it. Take a softer approach.

- Make sure your images are optimized so they load quickly. Your site needs to load within a second or two at most! Just tell your web developer that's what you need. https://developers.google.com/speed/pagespeed/

Reviews – In all honesty they can make or break your business. Here's what you NEED to know...

Simply put 'Reviews are vital to your online business'. You must get good reviews.

WHY?

Searchers want to see and use businesses that have lots of positive reviews. It gives them trust in your service and can give you a huge boost over your competitors.

In an extreme example which spa would you choose?

1 – Has 50+, 5 star reviews all raving about their service
2 – Has 3, 3 star reviews saying it was ok

What do you think most customers would choose when looking

at the reviews above? An extreme example perhaps, but it proves a point on how important reviews are.

How many products have you looked at on Amazon and then changed your mind because of the reviews, or decided on purchasing it after reading the reviews.

Reviews have a big role to play. Look at these stats:

74% of people will change their mind based on a bad review (Harris Interactive)
89% of people trust online reviews (Cone, Inc.)
92% of people read online reviews (Etailing group)

Almost 90% of people will do a search online before doing business.

Bad reviews or blog posts can seriously harm your business. So can a lack of presence or reviews online about your business. These customers will probably go to your competitors.

Whilst search engines may weigh the importance of reviews differently in their ranking algorithms when your site is displayed in the results with great reviews - as a visitor where would you click?

Reviews are not going away – people like seeing them. If you get great reviews it gives you a chance to show off - but equally, negative reviews can be very, very harmful. So do what you can to avoid getting them.

How search engines display reviews will change over time. But since visitors like them they will stay. If you can build up a bank of positive reviews it can massively help you overcome any negative reviews and help you stay in front of competitors.

Be warned of the low life...

Some low life competitors may leave negative reviews about your business as a way of trying to stop you from getting customers.

Unfortunately there isn't a lot that can be done unless you can 'prove' it was them trying to harm your business. That is one advantage to Yelp's system that it gives less importance to reviewers who have only left one or two reviews. But for other search engines that use a star system, if you only have one review and they gave you one star that can prove very harmful.

2HS

Phone: 0118 957 1713

Hours: Wednesday 10:00 am – 7:00 pm - See all

Reviews

4.4 ★★★★★ 6 Google reviews

More reviews: qype.co.uk, mylocalsalon.co.uk, findhairdresser.co.uk

You can see in this listing that this spa have 6 reviews. But click on '6 reviews' and you'll see:

4.4 ★★★★⯪ 6 reviews

A Google User
★★★★★ 2 years ago
Great Salon!!! I was really impressed with the at
and friendly and made me feel very relaxed. Ale:
and am really pleased with the ... More

A Google User
★★★★★ 2 years ago - ▣
I went here a couple of weeks ago and its the be
appointment my stylist actually took the time to
on the day of my appointment she was ... More

A Google User
★★★★★ 2 years ago
Went there recently and my stylist Rebecca wa
amazing all the team were very friendly and welc
was just as brilliant! I also had a hand ... More

A Google User
★★☆☆☆ 2 years ago
Uncomfortable Atmosphere for the price you pay
my hair.Altho the higlights weren't bad they were
past. whilst sitting in the salon i ... More

If you look in more detail you'll see what almost always happens. People tend to leave either 5 star reviews or 1 and 2 stars.

If that poor review had been first and followed by another poor review how do you think that would have affected their business? It could have been destroyed very quickly! People would lose trust and probably go elsewhere.

Where to get great 5 star reviews?

You'll want reviews from Google, as Google will clearly favour those since it has the data behind the people who wrote them (trust again).

But searching Google you can see that Google also displays other sites where you can have reviews. So you need to get reviews on these sites as well. Plus have a look at where your competitors have reviews; you'll want good reviews there as well.

In an ideal world you'll have good reviews on all the popular review sites rather than just one. It helps the search engines build up a picture of trust. If all your reviews were at one source you'd have to ask yourself why.

Google and other search engines need to trust reviews, otherwise it can harm their results. So they are doing what they can to spot fake positive and negative reviews. They are aware it happens and are trying to stop it.

Things they are likely to take into account – your review history, how many and what businesses you have reviewed in the past. Your location and the location of the business you reviewed, what words you used in the review, etc. People create fake accounts to leave both types of review.

You need good regular reviews in lots of places!

One idea that you may wish to try is after a customer leaves your spa you give them a 'thank you card' or something along those lines, perhaps with an offer for a future visit. But on that card have something along the lines of…

"We really hoped you enjoyed visiting our spa today and you'll return soon. We are trying hard to spread the word. As a small business it's hard competing against the big brands with their huge ad budgets. But one thing that would REALLY help us is if you would kindly leave us a review at websitename.com."

Here's the BIG TIP

Now the TIP here is you want that card or leaflet printed in about 6 different versions. BUT the only difference is where you ask people to leave a review e.g. on leaflet 1 you ask them to leave a review at Yelp, leaflet 2 could be TripAdvisor, etc.

It may also be worth adding "If for any reason you were not happy about your visit please contact us at … and give us the chance to correct it…."

Important - If you get any complaints here make sure you deal with them urgently and go over the top to make them happy. Send them flowers if you have to! Try and win that customer around.

Why - These people have your leaflet or email and have just read how to leave a review. Treat them like gold, even if it wasn't your fault! You could win round an angry customer and save a bad review.

Think of it this way if you send them a gift that costs you $50 and makes them happy, that would almost certainly save them from leaving a bad review that over the years could cost you far, far more!

Be Extra Smart…

If you are very smart, try and ask the customer earlier in conversation how they found you. "Oh did you see any reviews of us? On what site?" You then know what site they looked at and give them a leaflet with that website review name on. Chances are they may have an account there and are more likely to give you a review than if they had to set up new accounts.

Another TIP is if you already have their email address. If it's a Gmail address you can give them a Google review leaflet, if it's Yahoo give them a Yahoo leaflet, if another give them one of the more generic leaflets for Trip Advisor, etc.

Obviously if something didn't go quite right during the customer experience, don't give those customers a leaflet. Or try and remove their email from the mailing list. You don't want to give angry customers an easy way to leave a review!

You want to do what you can to encourage your good customers to leave a review within the rules. This is a great way of politely asking your happy customers and not the unhappy ones! Especially if you can show how their kind review will help a 'small family business'. People like helping local family businesses and you are just trying to encourage that.
For the cost of a few leaflets this is a great way to get positive reviews.

The almost FREE way to get reviews…

Alternatively you could use your follow up emails to ask for a review. You could say "…can you leave us a review at and then list 6 or seven addresses" or probably more effective (as most

107

people would probably leave a review at your first link) is to change the email once a week with a new review site.

In practice only a small percentage of your customers will leave reviews. Perhaps only 1 in 100. But they will build up over time. If you are doing more to encourage good reviews than your competitors, over time you should receive more trusted reviews than they do. It also makes it far harder for a competitor or poor review to damage your reputation.

1 bad review at the start is a 100 failure.
1 bad review after 99 good reviews is a 99% success rate.

Good reviews can equal more customers. They are that powerful.

Especially as some search engines also allow you to filter results by top reviewed. Unless you have lots of quality reviews you may never be featured and miss out.

That is why you need to start getting good reviews from your customers now. It will become harder and harder to compete against sites that have a bank of highly rated trusted reviews from lots of sources all spread out equally over time.

Don't try and cheat

Also be very careful about incentivising reviews, it is against the terms and conditions of many review sites. You don't want to get banned / removed for breaking their rules so make sure you read them!

Please DO NOT be tempted to go and buy reviews and set up fake profiles. You may not get caught straight away and it may

108

give you a boost to start with, but you are leaving your business in a dangerous situation. You are far better to do it correctly from the start.

Here's a BIG No No that many companies don't know

One thing to note – Do not have a computer set up in your business and ask customers to write a review as they leave. Sites track your computers IP address (a unique number given to your pc) and if 90% of your reviews come from one computer they are likely to be marked as fake and taken down. Your customers should leave reviews when they are at home or work.

You NEED to be doing this and actively seeking positive reviews. You are going to get reviewed on sites whether you like it or not! Remember the last time you had a bad experience with a company and how many people you told!

Don't believe me – Look at this FedEx Yelp review:

FedEx Home/Ground Delivery

★★★★★ 49 reviews   Rating Details

Category: Couriers & Delivery Services [Edit]

220 Shaw Rd
South San Francisco, CA 94080

+1-650-794-0490

49 reviews and only 1 and 2 stars!

You think of all the countless parcels that depot deliver on time each and everyday – hundreds and perhaps thousands! But did those customers post a review saying how great FedEx are? No

109

they only posted a review when things went wrong! They wanted to tell others and vent their frustration.

So since you are going to get negative reviews (like it or not) you NEED to be encouraging the GOOD ones as much as possible.

When that bad review does come

You are going to get bad reviews, it just happens. You can't please everyone all of the time. But try and take it as a learning opportunity so the same mistake / problem doesn't occur again.

If you can reply to the review do so, politely.

Leave a good reply acknowledging the problem and then say what you have done to address it so it doesn't happen again. I don't care if it wasn't your fault and the customer was a nightmare! Whatever you do, don't criticize the customer in your review. It looks unprofessional.

You can see how to respond to Google reviews here: https://support.google.com/places/answer/184271?hl=en&ref_topic=1656749

Use Google To Help You

You should monitor your reviews on all of your important review sites. The easiest way to do this is to use 'Google Alerts'. It's a fantastic, free resource from Google.

http://www.google.com/alerts

Alerts

Search query:	
Result type:	Everything ▼
How often:	Once a day ▼
How many:	Only the best results ▼

You can have Google do all the hard work for you and send you an email every time it finds a mention of your business.

You can set up more than one alert so you can use it to search for variations of your business name, your website address, or people in your business.

Bonus TIP – You can also use it to spot mentions of your competitors. Chances are you'll find out stuff about them online that they don't even know. If you spot reviews for them in places you haven't heard of, check them out and try and get reviews as well.

But you'll also find that you get notified if they were featured in an article on a website. If so contact the website and try to get yourself featured in another article later. It can be a great way to find great sites that are linking to your competitors.

If they can't or won't feature you then because they have just run a piece on your competitor simply make a note in your calendar and follow up with them in 6 months or a year.

If you do run into problems you can use various reputation management companies like Reputation.com who can try and help you correct them. But follow my advice and hopefully you won't need them.

You really need to do everything you can to get good quality reviews and lots of them. You know yourself when you've purchased products or experiences online you read the reviews of what you were looking to order.

A few negative reviews are fine providing you have lots of positive ones to compensate. In fact they make your profile look more genuine than just 4 or 5 reviews all gathered in a short time and no reviews since. You need good reviews collected regularly and try and minimize any negative ones!

By the way NEVER buy or incentivize reviews –

they are against the terms and conditions of almost every, if not all, review sites and if you are caught your listing could be permanently removed – thereby almost destroying your business. Imagine someone going to Yelp or Trip Advisor and there is no listing for you.

Here is what Trip Advisor say:

"Penalties will be given to properties that offer incentives to their guests for writing reviews. In all cases, reviews in question will be removed. Further penalties are given on a case-by-case basis and range from a warning to a red badge added to your property listing. The red badge warns prospective guests that a property has not adhered to TripAdvisor policy. It also significantly impacts the property's popularity ranking. - See more at: http://www.tripadvisor.co.uk/TripAdvisorInsights/n692/tripadvi

sors-incentives-policy-why-rewarding-traveler-reviews-against-rules#sthash.Pk2LzW3t.dpuf"

Google say:

"Reviews are only valuable when they are honest and unbiased. For instance, as a business owner or employee you should not review your own business or place of work. Don't offer money or product to others to write reviews for your business or write negative reviews about a competitor. We also discourage specialized review stations or kiosks set up at your place of business for the sole purpose of soliciting reviews. As a reviewer, you should not accept money or product from a business to write a review about them. Additionally, don't feel compelled to review a certain way just because an employee of that business asked you to do so. Finally, don't post reviews on behalf of others or misrepresent your identity or affiliation with the place you are reviewing."

Why not consider advertising on your competitors review page?

It's worth noting that you can advertise on many review sites as well. For example Yelp
https://biz.yelp.co.uk/support/advertising
allows you to advertise on your competitors listing (smart) and also to choose what review you would like at the top of your page (again very useful).

Can be very powerful

It's a great way to get your spa in front of your possible customers. If they are looking at the competition why not create a special 'Yelp' offer just for these people? They are highly targeted potential customers and currently looking at your competition. What can you do to tempt them over to you?

Come up with a great idea and the customer could be yours. Perhaps you could offer a bonus treatment, free gift (I would try and offer an 'extra bonus' rather than discounting your price).

Reviews truly can help make or break your business. Your customers are going to do it and you can't stop them. You just need to do your best to get more great reviews and try and stop any negative reviews.

If (and when) you do get a negative review where possible make sure you respond to it. Anyone looking at the reviews can still be persuaded to try your business. By the way be careful how you reply. There are countless articles on the web where reviews and responses have gone viral (spread quickly around the web and not always in a good way for the owner).

How do you reply to those bad reviews?

When you reply be as polite and friendly as you can. Always acknowledge any mistakes made and show how you have corrected them so that the same problem wouldn't occur again.

People need to know that you have understood the complaint.

Don't reply using foul language or accusing the customer of lying – or anything else that puts the customer in a bad light. Readers will think you may do the same to them and just be rude and arrogant! It's one of the biggest no no's.

In your reply just try to be as honest, open and genuine as you can be, acknowledge what the customer was complaining about

114

to show that you have understood and then explain fully what you have done to correct the issue so that other customers are not affected.

Try where possible not to get into posts going backwards and forwards between the two of you. Remember everyone can read these messages. Don't use 'big words' that make it look like you are talking down to your customer. Use regular everyday language.

When things do go wrong and it was your fault just be open and honest and say something like "I am truly very sorry for the ******, we simply made a huge error and I'm sorry you were affected. We are trying to find a solution right now so that no one else will experience ******. Unfortunately we are only human and mistakes, although thankfully very rarely, will happen. I would like to offer you and a friend a free treatment and I'll contact you privately to make arrangements. Thank you for your understanding and for letting me know about the problem. It is appreciated and sorry again."

Do this better than your competitor spa locations and you stand a great chance of winning more customers. All businesses will get good and bad feedback. You can't totally stop things going wrong. But when they do, acknowledge the problem and fix it straight away and above all take care of your customers; doing that will make you stand out.

The fact that you are reading this book puts you at a great advantage. Most spa shop owners are too focused on what's happening inside their business.

You understand that successful local marketing is vitally important as a massive boost to your business. I would strongly argue that time and money spent here is far more profitable than almost any other marketing you can do.

Getting your name known locally is hugely important. Get great reviews from word of mouth and on review sites and you've almost got it made.

That way your local customers know you are a great spa destination and anyone visiting the area and wanting a spa simply looks up your area name + spa and hopefully all they see are glowing reviews for you. Why would they want to go anywhere else?

Bonus TIP on Reviews

On your website make sure you create a page called "YourSpaName.com/Reviews" – This is a webpage that is totally controlled by YOU.

You can put whatever you want on this page so you want the best reviews and testimonials you can get. Get as many as you can.

One thing that works well is video testimonials. There is nothing like seeing and hearing a real customer talk about your business. They are really easy to do. You can record them on most smartphones or simply use a video camera. You just want to see the customer raving about your wonderful service.

Once you have the clip simply upload it to YouTube - https://www.youtube.com/upload (you'll need a Google account). They'll then give you a bit of code that you can put onto your website so that the video will play easily.

If you can't get a video ask your customer if you can simply take a photo to put with their testimonial. It's the next best thing and still really adds credibility to the testimonial.

Better than nothing is simply the testimonial and a name. But you really should try for either the video or at least a photo. They add a lot more weight and believability to the reader. You want to create as much trust as you can. It helps to start to create the relationship.

Using Online Marketing / Advertising For A Fast and Easy Way to Increase Customers

"Your goal is to be willing and able to spend more than your competitors to acquire customers. If you can do that... you win." Ryan Deiss

By putting everything else in place that you have learned in this book so far you should be in a position to do just that.

You know how to turn visitors into buyers and follow up for repeat sales. This should make each visitor far more valuable to you than they would be to your competitors.

Visit www.SpaBusinessMarketing.com for MORE expert advice

Providing you know your numbers you should now be able to bid more than your competitors to acquire customers.

If you can be the No. 1 result in Google for all the keywords that are relevant to you, you should get more chances to sell than all of your competitors.

Then the formula repeats:

More chances to sell – > – convert into customers – > – make more money than your competitors – > – gives you more money to acquire customers – > – more customers – > – bigger profits!

= You become one very happy spa owner!

You can start to see how important it is again to get everything else in place on your website:

- Capturing customer details
- Following up
- Product trip wire
- Acquire customers
- Follow up for repeat sales
- Get great reviews

Now you can do that better than your competitors go out and make the most of it. You can now buy highly targeted visitors.

Most of the search engines now allow you to target the keywords and phrases that you want to appear under. If you want to be found under 'Surrey Spa' you can be!

You can literally be the top result for that phrase today by using advertising. Imagine how many visitors you could get. All chances to sell.

Now before you rush off and set up your first advertising campaign on Google called 'Adwords' finish reading this guide. It is by no means definitive (there are good books on Amazon that fully explain Adwords better than I can here) but it should give you a good understanding and help stop you wasting your money, which Google make it surprisingly easy to do!

Using Adwords and the other online forms of advertising are certainly one of the fastest and most reliable ways to get customers.

If you can pay to get customers it puts you in a great position because you are less reliant on the search engines changing the way they rank pages. Yes overnight you could go from the No. 1 spot to nowhere and it's very hard to sort out.

Using advertising you can get customers quickly!

How to get started using Adwords to promote your local business

The Basics of Setting up Your First Google Adwords Campaign

Googling is now a verb in the English language. That alone should tell you that Google is the search engine you need to be concerned with when you want to mount an ad campaign online. It isn't enough to rely on SEO for your traffic; you need to get involved with running Google Adwords campaigns.

Adwords is based upon the old print style ads that you would buy and then select the circulation route that carried them. With Adwords, you use keywords to define the demographic markers of viewers you are trying to reach. You then bid on the keywords and that determines how many people see your ad, and how often. Because Adwords is all about data and demographics, you can create a highly profitable campaign for pennies on the dollar. This is why Adwords is gaining in appeal with new, small and local businesses. Especially with the rise of social media and mobile Internet browsing, you can do more for less to promote your business and products online with Google Adwords than ever before.

Let's get started. I will walk you through the process from keyword to campaign, and show you how to get the word out on social media, too!

First things first - Finding your keywords

Before you even go to the Adwords site, you need to have an idea about what keywords you are going to be using. Keywords are extremely important. They are what allow you and your customer to find each other. It isn't as easy as saying that you sell "spa treatments" and leave it at that. What if the latest trend is to call them "spa sessions"? If you are using one term and your customer is using another, you will wind up missing each other online.

It pays to sit and search for your own product. Use variations of the phrase, partial phrases and also look at forums where people who talk about the things you have to sell are commenting. You should also read the latest articles about your products and services that may not be in the usual industry reading material. All of this will help to increase the vocabulary you have to describe what you are offering. That is the basis of your keywords.

Once you have the list. Go to Adwords and get started.

Using General and Specific Keywords

The appeal of your keywords, or keyword type, boils down to either being general or specific. The keyword "spa" is general. Lots of different things can fall under the term spa. A "spa treatment" starts to get more specific and narrow its audience appeal. Whether you choose a general or specific keyword will depend on the goal you have for your ad.

If you want exposure and name recognition, start with general (which you almost certainly don't unless you have national reach). If you are specialized and/or local, stay with specific keywords.

Below is a general table for someone who focuses on 'spas' and how they develop their specific keywords from the general keyword at the top.

Spa Business Marketing Strategies

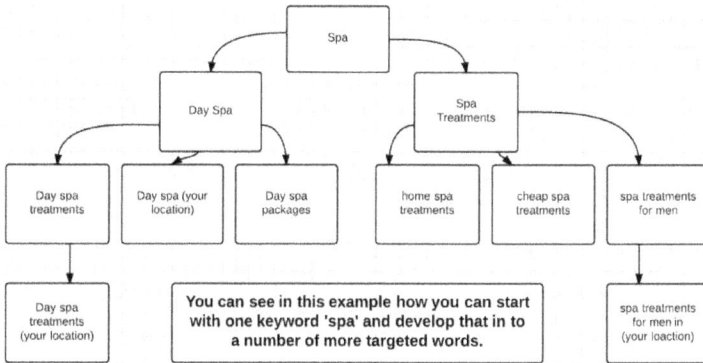

General terms will get you general views. Global terms will get you views from all over the globe. Since you are selling very specific services you only want visitors from a certain location.

One of the things that Google uses to rank the placement of your ads is the average score it receives based upon the number of views and clicks. This contributes to your overall Quality Score.

If your spa treatments are being shown to millions and millions of people all over the world, but only 0.00001% click on them because your ad says "Don't click unless you live in East Chepeepee USA" Google won't see that as a successful ad and will lower your score. Too low a score and your ad doesn't get seen!

Geo-targeting keywords

This is a very fancy term for not wasting your ad budget on showing pictures of your spa (if you only sell in Denver) to someone in Anchorage. By adding in a location specific keyword, like "Denver" you can eliminate people searching in Anchorage. This doesn't mean that only people who search for "best spas Denver" are going to be shown your ad, it means that when

Google detects that the person searching for "spas" is in Denver, they may see your ad, too.

Make sure you read the 'locations and languages' section in about 8 pages. It can save you wasting lots of money!

The Adwords Keyword Tool

Even if you have a list of keywords that you are sure will be perfect for your ads, it pays to use the Google Adwords Keyword, too. This tool not only will help you come up with even more ideas for keywords, it will show you a report about the competitiveness for the keyword and its average cost.

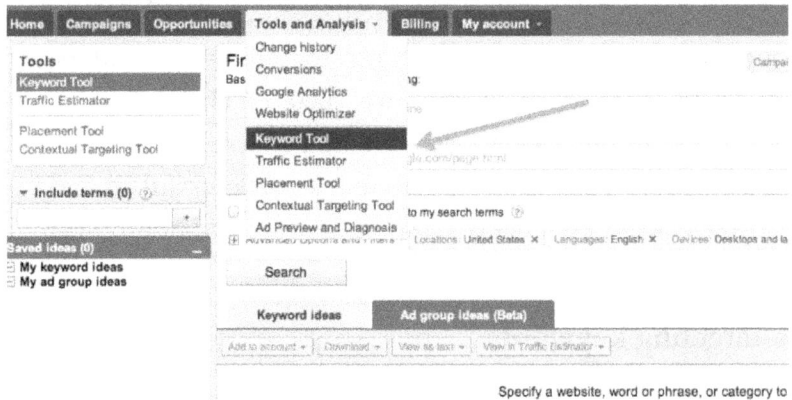

Type in the keywords you want to search for and hit enter. Google then will generate a keyword report listing the best 3 keywords of your whole list. They will also provide a list of keyword suggestions at the bottom of the report.

Keyword ideas	Ad group ideas (Beta)				About this data

Add to account ▾	Download ▾	View as text ▾	View in Traffic Estimator ▾	Sorted by Relevance ▾	Columns ▾

▼ ✓ Save all Search terms (3)				1 - 3 of 3 ▾ ‹ ›

Keyword	Competition	Global Monthly Searches	Local Monthly Searches	Approximate CPC (Search)
patio furniture ▾	High	1,220,000	823,000	$1.82
lawn chairs ▾	High	49,500	40,500	$1.13
outdoor seating ▾	High	27,100	22,200	$1.81

+ ✓ Save all **Lawn Chairs (27)** - folding lawn chairs, plastic lawn chairs, lawn chair...	More like these
+ ✓ Save all **Furniture Sale (8)** - patio furniture sale, patio furniture on sale...	More like these
+ ✓ Save all **Furniture Discount (7)** - discount patio furniture, discounted patio furniture...	More like these
+ ✓ Save all **Patio Furniture Outdoor (9)** - outdoor patio furniture, outdoor patio furniture sets...	More like these
+ ✓ Save all **Furniture Sets (8)** - patio furniture sets, cheap patio furniture sets...	More like these
+ ✓ Save all **Wicker Furniture (14)** - wicker patio furniture, wicker patio furniture clearance...	More like these
+ ✓ Save all **Outdoor Furniture (47)** - outdoor furniture, contemporary outdoor furniture...	More like these
+ ✓ Save all **Cushion (43)** - patio furniture cushions, outdoor cushions, patio cushions...	More like these
+ ✓ Save all **Teak Furniture (5)** - teak patio furniture, teak outdoor furniture, teak furniture...	More like these
+ ✓ Save all **Outdoor Patio (6)** - outdoor patio, outdoor patio chairs, outdoor patio sets...	More like these

Looking at it column by column

 In the top left column you can see the three keyword terms you entered. The results for the keywords are then shown across the columns.

- Second column – this shows you the rate of competition for your keywords. The rate of competition means how many advertisers are bidding on the word. The more bidders, the higher the cost of the keyword.
- Third and fourth columns – global and monthly averages of searches for keywords over the past 12 months. Make sure that if you are a locally focused business you are paying attention to the right column. The column will also show your country and language, too.
- Last column – these are estimated cost-per-click (CPC) for the keywords. This is based on an average Google figures from estimating the cost of the click to your landing page from each ad.

125

Below the columns is a list of keyword suggestions generated that relate to the keywords you entered. Just because they relate does not always mean they are relevant. While you do want to choose as many relevant keywords as possible to increase your potential bid, you don't want active bids out on keywords that are ineligible for auction. An ineligible keyword means no one is looking for it so it is not worth anything. If you have keywords like those, it can bring down the score of your site.

Negative Keywords

Negative keywords refer to keywords that are so descriptively close to what is relevant to your business that they could easily be confused as referring to yours. An example would be a similarly named or spelled company or product. By listing the negative keywords you will avoid losing ad exposure to people who wouldn't click on it anyway. Don't think you will gain conversion from trying to be mistaken for something else either. Set your negative keywords and focus on attracting the people who will want what you have to offer.

Traffic Estimator Tool

The Traffic Estimator Tool is one of the best things that you can use to determine the maximum cost per click (CPC) you can afford that will also give you the best return on your campaign. It can take some practice and scratch paper to really figure out what the daily CPC means in hard cash to your budget so make sure that you have a good grasp of the absolute figure first, and back it up with a monthly spending cap, to prevent yourself from going over budget while you are still learning the process.

Once in the traffic estimator, type in your desired keywords and click ' Get Estimates.' Here you will not see any data until entering a max CPC and daily budget. This allows you to determine the optimal CPC and budget for the number of impressions or clicks that you are looking for based upon the budget you have to spend.

Making a profit with click through

Here is a basic example of what it takes to make a profit from a click through. Let's say that you have a $2 max CPC for a campaign. Your daily budget is $600 for your entire company.

- That $2 CPC nets you 532-650 daily clicks, and 6,626 to 8,099 impressions.
- For every 20 clicks, you are making one $50 sale.
- That means on a daily basis, you are making a $10 profit on your budget spend.

127

To make sure that your CPC keeps returning a profit, you need to look at the average position of your ad (Avg. Pos.).

	Draft campaign	Daily Clicks	Daily Impr.	Avg. Pos.
	Draft campaign (1 ad groups, 2 keywords)	591.25	7,362	1.4
	My keyword ideas (2) edit	591.25	7,362	1.4
	lawn furniture	77.54	1,080	1.4
	outdoor chairs	513.71	6,282	1.4

The average position tells you where in the search results pages your ad will appear. Positions 1-8 are usually on the first page, and therefore are seen most frequently.

The click-through rate (CTR) refers to the percentage of people who clicked on the ad. Bear in mind that the average CTR rate is 2% depending on product, industry and company so don't stress if you aren't getting above a 10. The CTR shown in the example below is very good.

	Draft campaign	Daily Clicks	Daily Impr.	Avg. Pos.	Daily Cost	CTR
	Draft campaign (1 ad groups, 2 keywords)	591.25	7,362	1.4	$592.36	8%
	My keyword ideas (2) edit	591.25	7,362	1.4	$582.36	8%
	lawn furniture	77.54	1,080	1.4	$73.52	7.2%
	outdoor chairs	513.71	6,282	1.4	$518.84	8.2%

Now that you have some solid reasons for picking the best keywords for your ads, it is time to create your Google Adwords campaign.

Creating a Google Adwords Campaign

Google Adwords allows you to create many campaigns, and each campaign consists of ad groups. Each ad group consists of keywords that are all related to a similar topic, and they can contain as many ads as you want that rotate among the keywords you have. This rotation can be based on clicks, conversion rates, or evenly distributed among your various ad groups within a campaign.

Create your campaign

Creating your first campaign is easy. A large window will appear and you click on the choice to start a new campaign.

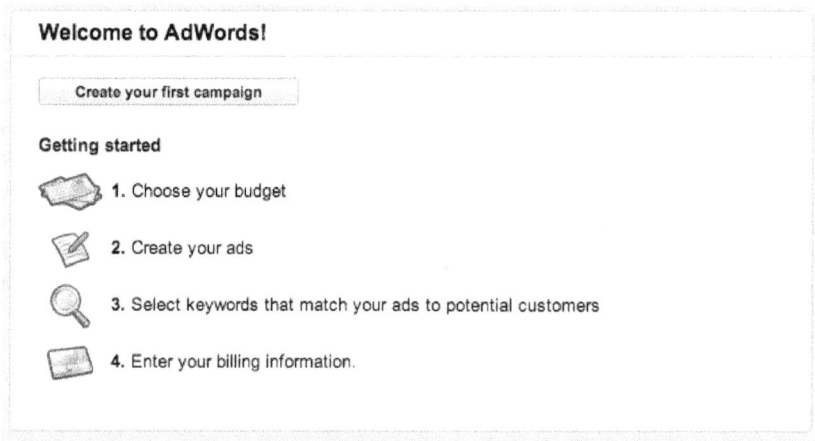

Welcome to AdWords!

Create your first campaign

Getting started

1. Choose your budget

2. Create your ads

3. Select keywords that match your ads to potential customers

4. Enter your billing information.

Pick the campaign type you want

There are many options for your campaign settings but the most important are as follows:

- **Default:** This is the best choice to get the most exposure fast and raise your CTR. Your ads will go out on Google Networks and affiliates. It may not have a good return on CMA or acquisition.

- **Search Network Only:** Ads will be placed on search results and Google network search sites such as Google Maps, Images, Shopping and AOL. This option provides you with more control and more limited exposure, but it can be most effective for targeting specific geographic locations.

- **Display Network Only:** Ads will be placed on Google Display Network websites such as YouTube and Gmail only.

- **Display Network Only:** This is the best choice if you are seeking to follow up with people that have already come to your site or clicked on an ad earlier. It will redisplay the ad for them.

- **Search and Display Networks (Mobile Devices):** If your product, service or business is designed for people who are most likely to be looking for it using a mobile device then this is the most appropriate choice.
- **Online Video:** This will tell Google to place your ad on Display Network video sites that are relevant (such as YouTube).

Locations and Languages

Name the campaign something relevant. Next, you want to determine in what location your ad will appear. If your product or service can be sold anywhere, selecting a broad reach is fine, such as "All Country and Territories," or "United States and Canada."

Since you will probably have a location-specific service, you can choose where your ad will appear and see exactly how many people your ad will reach in your location. Using both this and geographic targeting within your ads, Google will optimize your ads to only appear for people that are within your target market.

You can further specify your results by entering locations that you want to exclude from your search; meaning people from a certain location will never be able to see your ad.

You then will want to choose the language your customers speak. This will not translate the ad into another language, but it will place ads on search results for people who have selected this language as their primary language. For example, if you choose Spanish as the language your customers speak, a person who has selected Spanish as their primary language in Google will see your ad when they use the search engine, but the ad will still be in the language in which you wrote it.

Networks and Devices

The next option you have is the ability to customize the networks and options that your ad will be shown on. You can go with an automated setting, but customizing has its benefits. You can also change these settings at any time.

Networks and devices

Networks ⑦ ○ All available sites (Recommended for new advertisers)
◉ Let me choose...
Search ☑ Google search
☑ Search partners (requires Google search)
Display ☑ Display Network ⑦
◉ Broad reach: Show ads on pages that match my primary targeting method ⑦
Example: Show ads if keywords match
○ Specific reach: Show ads only on pages that match all my targeting methods ⑦
Example: Show ads only if both keywords and placements match

Devices ⑦ ○ All available devices (Recommended for new advertisers)
◉ Let me choose...
☑ Desktop and laptop computers
☑ Mobile devices with full browsers
☑ Tablets with full browsers
⊞ Advanced mobile and tablet options

Here are the options explained in more detail.

- **Search Partners:** This can increase exposure through promoting your ads on partner networks of Google.

- **Display Network:** This term refers to networks that are specifically owned or affiliated with Google.

- **Broad Reach:** If any of your keywords, in any order, appear in a search your ad may be shown.

This can increase exposure but may not accurately target your demographic.

- **Specific Reach:** A specific reach means there must be more of an exact match between the keywords searched and yours before your ad is shown. If your product is very specific to a market, this may be a good choice to make.
- **Devices:** This choice determines whether your ad will be shown to views detected to be accessing the Internet via mobile devices, desktops or other means.

Bidding and Budget

There is more information on handling bidding and bid adjustments in the section on creating a strategy later in this book. Here are the basics that you need to understand when first starting out.

The three main terms you need to know are:

1. CPC: This option, cost-per-click, only charges you when someone clicks on your ad. This is a good option if you are focused on increasing traffic to your website.
2. CPM: Cost per thousand impressions is used in the display network. This is helpful if you are looking to get your ad and brand in front of as many people as possible.
3. CPA: Cost per acquisition charges you when the person who clicked on your ad converts, often into a sale. This

can be used with conversion tracking and other applications.

These determine what you are paying for. It is important to remember that the cost of any of these can change according to the time of day, and the day per week that you are bidding on. What will determine which of these options you should choose for your campaign isn't just your budget; but how you need viewers to interact with you online. For example, if you just need to get your brand out there – CPM is best. CPC is what many people use in the beginning so they can more accurately test their ads' appeal to their demographic. CPA is usually more expensive but works well when you have a solid campaign developed.

As far as budgeting, one of the benefits of Adwords is you can set monthly caps and limits so that you do not go over budget. It will take a while for you to have enough data to really determine what is the best budget and approach for you. Using the Traffic Estimator is an invaluable tool when trying to determine what type of budget you will need to see a profit from your campaigns.

Advanced Settings

The Advanced Settings option allows you more control over the customization of your campaign through settings such as scheduling, demographics and capping and more.

Schedule

Based upon a review of your performance data you will be able to determine on what time and what days your ads receive more clicks. There is more about why this is important when it comes to the strategy section in this book. Basically, once you notice that there is a time when you perform better or worse with an ad, click on Schedule and then Edit to select the times and days your ad will run.

There is a lot that can influence the time and days that are appropriate for your ad. By reading up more on the demographic of your users, and reviewing your performance reports – you can very closely determine your maximum viewing times. It is important that the people viewing you are in your demographic. Don't just go for maximum viewing by anyone.

Ad schedule   ⊠

Edit days and times below. When you're happy with the schedule, click "Save." To bid more or less during particular time periods, switch to the bid adjustment mode. (You can always switch back.)

Reset to all days and hours   Mode: Basic | **Bid adjustment** | Clock: **12 hour** | 24 hour

Day	Time period	% of bid	Midnight	4:00 AM	8:00 AM	Noon	4:00 PM	8:00 PM
Monday	08:00 PM - 10:00 PM	100%						■■
Tuesday	08:00 PM - 10:00 PM	100%						■■
Wednesday	08:00 PM - 10:00 PM	100%						■■
Thursday	08:00 PM - 10:00 PM	100%						■■
Friday	08:00 PM - 10:00 PM	100%						■■
Saturday	Paused all day							
Sunday	Paused all day							

America/New_York

Save   Cancel

Settings for delivery, capping and location

Google Adwords allows you to set some automated choices to better present your ads and to determine which of your ads is most successful.

Optimize for Clicks: This is an automated setting that allows Adwords to select which ads to show based upon the projected percentage of clicks they will receive. This is good in the beginning, but as you learn more about your campaigns you don't want anything automated about selecting which ads are shown.

Optimize for Conversions: If the name of the game is conversions and not traffic, use this setting to see which of your ads does better.

Rotate Evenly: You can set up a schedule for rotating ads through your monthly plan so you can see how they do at different times. This is ideal for testing out ad ideas to see what works best.

Frequency Capping: This is a very important setting to take advantage of to increase effectiveness. Frequency capping means you can pre-set a limit for how often someone is going to see your ad. This is important because after 5 or so views, the ad has lost its window of opportunity with the viewer. By removing it from view, but coming back to allow it to be reviewed again within the next cycle – you can increase your potential for action.

Demographic limits

If your ad is using the display network then you can set limits to what demographics your ad is shown to. Only display network ads can see a group report of the demographics of their users, which is why there is this restriction. Demographic limitations can be very useful when you have a product or service that is targeted towards a specific age group or gender, or that your reports show only appeals to a specific age group or gender.

Demographic exclusions and reporting

This summary shows how your ads have performed on sites that offer demographic data. You can prevent your ads from showing to a specific demographic group by excluding the group below.

0.00% of total impressions are from sites with demographic data.

Traffic Reports by Gender and Age (for last 7 days)

Gender	Exclude	Clicks	Impr.	CTR	Avg. CPC	Cost
Male	☑	0	0	0.00%	$0.00	$0.00
Female	☐	0	0	0.00%	$0.00	$0.00
Undetermined		0	0	0.00%	$0.00	$0.00

Age	Exclude	Clicks	Impr.	CTR	Avg. CPC	Cost
18-24	☑	0	0	0.00%	$0.00	$0.00
25-34	☑	0	0	0.00%	$0.00	$0.00
35-44	☑	0	0	0.00%	$0.00	$0.00
45-54	☐	0	0	0.00%	$0.00	$0.00
55-64	☐	0	0	0.00%	$0.00	$0.00
65+	☐	0	0	0.00%	$0.00	$0.00
Undetermined	☐	0	0	0.00%	$0.00	$0.00

Save   Cancel

Adwords is set up to allow you to integrate your ads with social media, specifically Google+. Using the Social Settings options you can give a way for viewers to engage with your ad by using the +1 button and sharing the ads as well. This is one of the easiest ways to generate more presence on line, gain referrals and create retention.

Visit www.SpaBusinessMarketing.com for MORE expert advice

⊟ Social settings

+1 on Display Network ⑦   ⦿ Include the +1 button and the +1 annotations on my ads on the Display Network.
Display Network only   ◯ Do not include the +1 button and the +1 annotations on my ads on the Display
Network.

⊟ Keyword matching options

Exact and phrase match ⑦   ⦿ Include plurals, misspellings, and other close variants
Search Network only   ◯ Do not include close variants

Create the Ad Group

All the Ad Group means is a way for you to remember what the campaign is later and to allow you to organize your ads and campaigns. Think of an Ad Group as a folder in a directory. This is why making sure that the name of the ad group is relevant to your keywords used in the campaign is so important.

Create ad group

Name this ad group

An ad group contains one or more ads and a set of related keywords. For best results, try to focus all the ads and keywo this ad group on one product or service. Learn more about how to structure your account.

Ad group name: outdoor chairs

Once you name your ad group then you can create the type of ad copy you want. You can use the Google Display ad builder to build from a library of templates, or you can create unique ad content – including video ads. Ad options include text, image or mobile.

The text of an ad allows you a title that is 25 characters long and two lines of text with 35 characters for each line.

For effective text ads they must have the following three things.

138

1. **Keyword Relevance** – relevance affects your overall Quality Score. It is based on how well your ad copy relates to your keywords.

2. **Call-to-action (CTA)** – Make sure your ad includes a direct call to action such as "call us today!" or "learn more" that is also connected to a link maximized to allow the viewer to take that action.

3. **Value** – Your ad should let the viewer know what value you have to offer them.

Easier in real life than you think

The entire process to set up a Google Adwords account campaign is simple and intuitive. Google has made it a step-by-step process that is easy for you to walk through. Once you have the basics set up, it's time to learn more about the details of strategizing and maximizing the effectiveness of your campaigns.

Adwords Marketing Strategies for Local Businesses

Now that you have an Adwords account it is time to form a strategy for how to use it effectively. The single most common mistake that people make with their Adwords accounts is that they set them up, select an automated bid adjustment plan, put in a few keywords and then never revisit the account.

If you are going to make Adwords work for you, you have to dedicate time to the management and review of the performance of the account. Everything in Adwords is going to affect your CTR and Quality Score rating. Both of those are going to affect the placement and effectiveness of your ads.

Here are the basics of creating a strategy to guide the management of your account.

Account Structure

Since you have a local business, you should be focusing your account structure on a specific location. This means that a part of your Adwords should include a specific location name that is recognizable. While it may seem like it would be better to offer spa treatments to the whole world because you sell oils, etc. all over, adding "spa treatments denver" to your main structure is going to land you a higher CTR and quality score.

Don't rely on an IP address to provide you with the location identification for searches and placements. Many times the IP address reflected has nothing to do with the location of your business. You have to stack the deck in your favour by making sure to include these terms specifically. To do so, open up the Adwords Editor and add the location name to all of your keywords. What you will gain from it will far outweigh the minimum cost of adding the word in.

Bid on your own Brand Name

For some reason this is the one thing that people forget to do. If you have ever read stories about celebrities or companies having to buy their own name online, a large part of it stems from the same kind of thinking that allows you to forget to bid on your own brand name. When you think about it there is no reason why you shouldn't make this your primary bid, especially if you are a small business with a limited budget.

There is no keyword more relevant to you than your own brand name. Based upon local brick and mortar and pavement marketing you are going to have a higher rate of visitors who are directly searching for your brand name than a term. This will help you to boost your CTR and quality score quickly.

The Modified Broad Match

Adwords allows you to identify broad match keywords by adding a plus symbol (+) to the front of any individual word in

141

the keyword string. This functions much the same as doing a search in your file manager using the asterisk (*) symbol after the word. It tells Google this word must be part of the search query. The keyword can then be triggered by any search term which

- Has words marked with the plus symbol
- Has any/none of the other keywords
- Is in any order
- Is a recognized misspelling of the term
- Is the plural form of the word

If Google marks the keyword you want to use as ineligible, try using the modified broad match method to increase chances of relevance in the search.

Using the modified broad match is also a good way to boost your quality score when you first start a campaign. It will show you as more relevant to more searches and raise your CTR. Later, as you begin to refine your campaigns and have solid performance data for analysis you will want to use the broad match less as it can then swing to a negative influence as well. Too many hits with no follow through can lower your score.

> **TIP** - The modified broad match can provide you with a cheaper way to explore the viability of new keywords.

Bidding Strategy

The one thing that you need to remember about building a successful Bidding Strategy is the word "building." Google offers automated bidding strategies, which may be tempting when you are first starting out, but you should never use them.

The reason for this is that every business is unique. Automated strategies are boilerplate strategies that won't adjust for your target locations and demographics. Although you can go in and custom tweak the boiler plate, it will save you much time and money in the end if you begin from scratch and build a custom strategy of your own.

Campaigns	Adgroups
Device	Device
Location	Topics
Time of day (ad scheduling)	Interests
	Remarketing lists
	Placements

Bid Adjustments

Bid Adjustments allow you to do more than just adjust the cost of expenditure on an ad. By using the analytic reports and tracking your CTR performance, you can increase your Quality Score through Bid Adjustments. These adjustments allow you to target your bids to maximize what you know to be true about your target traffic's context, devices, location and the time and day that they are searching for what you have to offer.

Location Bid Adjustments

+ Locations	Set bid adjustment	Delete
☐ Location	Campaign	↓ Bid adj. ?
Total		
☐ New Jersey,		+ 10%

Location Bid Adjustments are important because Google uses them in factoring the Quality Score for your entire account. The best way to review them is to click on the Dimensions tab and review the CTR performance. Where you are performing poorly, you want to increase the bid amount until there is a stable performance level. If they do not respond quickly (in a day), you may want to consider eliminating those areas until you can rethink your strategy to avoid their bringing down your Quality Score.

What is important to remember is that all of these bids and adjustments will reflect back quickly to your analytics, but they will take a few days before they will begin to be reflected in your Quality Score. You have to make a dedicated effort to stay on top of your Adwords management to get the best results.

Scheduling Bid Adjustments

This is something that most people get wrong. They know that by reading their performance reports they can tell what times of day, or days that their ads are not doing well. The typical response is to then lower the bid amount during those times. This is the wrong approach because it still leaves your business with a poorly performing bid that will deliver bad CTR and lower the overall Quality Score.

A better approach is to identify the times when your ads are not performing and remove the bids altogether. Better to have to run a risk of having to bid slightly more, but maintain your CTR and Quality Score overall.

Device Bid Adjustments

You can set your mobile bid adjustments at the ad group level to make sure that your ads will only reach mobile users if they, in turn, can reach your site. This isn't a matter of connectivity but a question of whether or not a mobile user can use your site. If your site includes coding such as Flash, or has a design that isn't mobile friendly – you are just going to frustrate users and waste your money on reaching people who can't reach back.

You can review your CPC reports to see what traffic is coming off of mobile ads and make adjustments accordingly.

Weather Bid Adjustments

This is just a fancy term for Adwords Scripts. This is where you will find all the things that you wish Adwords did, like send you alerts on caps and setting up automatic processes. Using scripts can save you an awful lot of time and money by taking care of what you already know will happen.

One of the reasons they are called "weather bids" is that you can actually set up a script to monitor the weather and adjust your bids accordingly. For instance, if you run an outdoor event service, during a spate of bad weather you want to decrease your bid because no one is going to be looking for your service. When the weather is good, you want to increase your bid to maximize your reach to people who are looking for what you have to offer.

Google Analytics Bid Adjustments Report

An important metric to review is the Bid Adjustment report. This can let you know more information about how successful your bids have been in effecting traffic and conversion rates. You can find this report as an option in the Advertising area of Google Analytics. It will break down how your traffic behaved in relation to the bid adjustments you put in place.

Keeping your Average Position

Draft campaign	Daily Clicks	Daily Impr.	Avg. Pos.
Draft campaign (1 ad groups, 2 keywords)	591.25	7,362	1.4
My keyword ideas (2) edit	591.25	7,362	1.4
lawn furniture	77.54	1,080	1.4
outdoor chairs	513.71	6,282	1.4

You have to maintain your Average Position in order to make sure that your account is cost effective. This is non-negotiable for small businesses with limited budgets. It is important to bear in mind that the displayed position isn't your true average position. The displayed position doesn't reflect the eligibility of your ads to run. If you are not mindful of which of your keywords are not currently eligible for auction, then they can bring down your Quality Score.

To avoid this, add a column to your keyword spreadsheet so you can track "Lost Impression Share Due to Rank." If your keywords are losing impressions then they are in danger of losing eligibility to show. If they are still relevant and your Quality Score is good, you may have to increase your bids at the keyword level to keep them from negatively affecting you. The golden rule is to do this if you see a 5% loss in impression shares on a specific keyword.

Controlling your Ad Spend

Adwords allows you to set a monthly billing cap to help control your spending during the monthly billing cycle. This is highly recommended if paying attention to cost is important to your budget. However, bear in mind that when you do reach your cap, your ads will just stop showing and you will receive no notice unless you manually set up the provided script to send you an alert.

Bespoke Location Landing Pages

Bespoke bears mentioning because their landing pages have a proven track record for improving conversion rate and your

Quality Score. You can create a landing page for each product or service area you have an offer in. Make sure the keywords are relevant to your location and your user search terms.

Ad Extensions

Once you have gotten your account in order so that you have a strong Quality Score and average position it is time to turn your attention to maximizing the use of Ad Extensions. Ad Extensions can radically increase user engagement and CTR and don't cost any more than the average click.

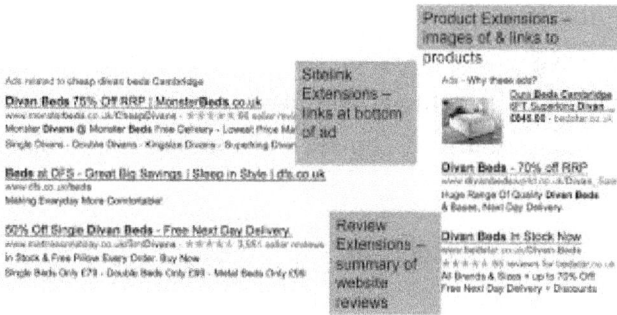

The following are the most important extensions to use for your business to attract local traffic.

Review Extensions

Review extensions are still in the beta phase but you want to make sure you jump on them when they are released for trial use. They will allow your business to show a preview of a review with your ad that links to a review site. The click through doesn't cost you anything. It is paid for by the review site.

Email Extensions

You have to contact your Adwords Rep to set up email extensions since doing so will require changes to your Privacy Policy. Email extensions offer an exchange to visitors – in exchange for their email address, they will get something from you (a free eBook, newsletter or discount for example). This has become an increasingly popular way to generate good analytics.

Image Extensions

Make sure you review and follow the relevancy guidelines set by Adwords when doing image extensions. This provides a way for you to attach information to images that applies to your ad group and then will show in searches.

Offer Extensions

Offer extensions are direct offers to viewers. They are easy to set up and text based so it is faster to create changing offers as well. Offers will also show up in search listings. Don't think you don't have anything to offer – it could be anything from a site evaluation to a discount coupon to an article about something you know your demographic will be interested in.

Using Twitter Marketing for your Local Business

While everyone knows that social media marketing is the way to go with your local business, a lot of the social media sites just take too much time to use. That is the advantage of Twitter.

The short style messages, and the ability to upload pictures, add links and video all from a smartphone or your laptop make it the ideal on-the-go tool. For local businesses, it can provide a much needed platform to talk to local consumers and get on the map in your area.

The idea

The idea with using Twitter for your business isn't to get a ton of people following you and then rain tweets on them like a storm, it's all about getting a few people in your area engaged with you online so that they retweet your tweets to their followers, or mention your business frequently.

What this does

This is something called social proof. While you can blast out links and tweets to followers, most of them will be ignored. Why? Because you are a business and a business wants to sell things – ergo – you will be perceived as someone trying to make a buck. When someone that someone knows and respects mentions a business, it is a sign that they think the business is worth looking into or supporting. You want this "social proof" that you are about more than the bottom dollar to build loyalty.

Local loyalty with customers is the key to long-term success. It may sound funny but the short and fast world of Twitter is about creating a long-term relationship with customers, not a short one-time encounter.

Finding out who you want to get noticed by

Twitter has a great feature called the "Advanced Search"

https://twitter.com/search-advanced

which is a goldmine for a local business looking to make real local connections. You can open up this feature and search for tweets based upon keywords and location.

This is how you can find out who is looking for what you sell in your area. This is a very proactive form of marketing. Rather than relying on customers using the advanced search to find you, use it to find them and then follow them.

Make sure to use the "Save this search" option so you can run your searches periodically to check for new connection

151

possibilities. Just because a search didn't return a hit the first time doesn't mean that no one in the area is trying to find what you do – you have to keep checking. What makes it even easier is that when you save your searches they will automatically be placed under the "Searches" tab on your homepage.

Find your Top Local Tweeters

If you want to get mentioned by people who matter in your local area, you have to find out who your top local tweeters are. There are a few different ways to do this. The first is slow and painful. You can follow people and then look at the people they follow and then watch your stream to see who posts a lot and is retweeted a lot. You can also look on the left side of your homepage for the automatic suggestions from Twitter – but not all of them will be relevant to you, or even from your area.

Or, you can use one of the many apps that are designed to let you look at the rankings of different Twitter accounts by geographic location and for different keywords and so on.

The ranking apps

There are four main apps that exist that are considered to be reliable indicators of top twitter accounts of local areas.

- Tweet Grader – https://marketing.grader.com/ is a quick and dirty app that ranks cities by the amount of registered Twitter accounts in the population. Click on the city name and there is a "Twitter Elite" list that will show which of those accounts is the most active.

- WeFollow – wefollow.com This app is very similar to TweetGrader but they have more of an emphasis on trying to limit their counts to active users.
- Twitter Counter – TwitterCounter.com this app provides the "must follow" lists of the top 100 active Twitter users. Make sure that you aren't looking at the global list but choose the specific city you need. The option for that is at the bottom of the page.
- Followerwonk – Followerwonk.com This app works like Twitter Counter and all the rest but it lets you search their lists using keywords as well. This can not only help you identify people who may be a good idea for you to follow but businesses in the area as well. One aspect that businesses tend to overlook is that if you follow an associated business you will attract followers to you as well (such as a tire business following an auto parts dealer).

Use mapping apps

Bing has a mapping system similar to Google Maps but the difference is they will also register Twitter users registered in that area as well.

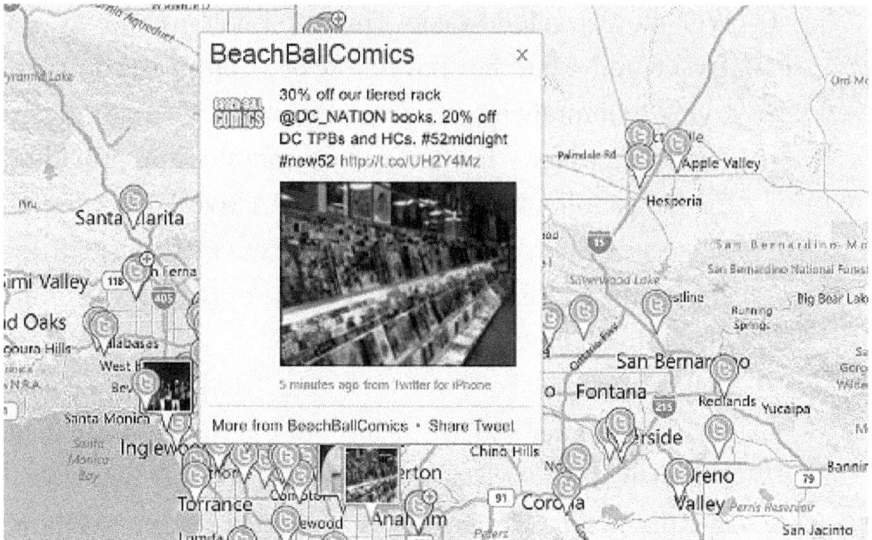

To use this feature go to the "Select Maps" option on the top tabs and select "Twitter Maps." This will show you a visual location in the area of top Twitter users and top local businesses mentioned by them.

You can also search the Twitter map by keyword to narrow down your results even more. Click on the link to see the tweets and then follow the person who posted them.

All of these apps show that the more you tweet quality messages, the more active you will be perceived and the more people will retweet and mention your business. This is why using Twitter is essential to your business. It doesn't take a full cost campaign to make some local connections that will increase your reach with ease.

Putting Adwords into Facebook

Facebook has created two different kinds of pages for their users. There are 'personal' pages and 'fan' pages. Fan pages are pages that represent businesses, venues, causes, organizations, artists and anything else you can be a fan of. What confuses many business owners is that fan pages are the business pages on Facebook.

Part of the evolution of online commerce has been its constant redefinition on social networking sites. While some sites offer specific business accounts, Facebook went with fan pages as it requires businesses to have a personal account, too. Facebook recognized early on that people are more responsive to businesses online that also have a personal face. You may be Motofire Tires in the business world, but first you are John Moto. By tying in the personal to the business, Facebook is letting businesses tap into an online marketing phenomenon referred to as "social proof." With social proof, it is the public's perception

155

of the integrity and character of the person that fuels their loyalty to the business or product.

Fan pages are easy to set up, easy to use and an incredible local marketing tool. The more you can get fans to like your page, the more traffic you will see to your website and/or store.

How to set up a Fan Page

Setting up a Facebook Fan Page is simple, and one of the most effective ways to reach out and connect with local consumers to promote your business. You use it to build awareness, advertise, promote and gather support.

Here are the basics of getting a Fan Page up and running. It is broken down into two parts. The first part lists the 7 steps involved to create a fan page.

Step 1 – Sign in to your account. If you don't have an account, sign up for one. It is free and easy to do. You will need an active email account to do so. If you already have an account, just sign in as you normally would.

Step 2 – Click on "Settings." At the upper right hand corner of the page there is a small icon that looks like a gear. Click on this to open up the settings menu for your account.

Step 3 – Select "Advertising." Under the settings menu, select the "Advertising" option and click on it.

Step 4 – Select "Create a Page." You have to look to the left of the screen, near the centre and you will see an option to "create a page." Click on this.

156

Step 5 – Select the type of page to create. Here you have six different choices for the type of page you want to create. They are all fan pages, but geared towards different types of entities.

1. Local business or place: This applies to businesses or organizations with a local place. You will need to also select the type of business that you are and enter in your physical address.

2. Company, organization or institution: You will need to select which you are (company, organization or institution) and enter in the name. This differs from the local business choice as it implies you have more than one location.

3. Brand or product: If you want to create a fan page for a unique brand identity or single product, choose this option. You will then be asked to categorize the product and enter in the name.

4. Artist, band, or public figure: This is where the "fan" part really comes into play. You can create a fan page for any artist, band or public figure with or without their consent. You will choose their category and enter in their name.

5. Entertainment: This page can be trickier as it can be a basic "fan" page of a type of entertainment (film, TV show etc.) or it can be used to promote a

venue as well.

6. <u>Cause or community name:</u> Type in the name of the cause or community name.

Step 6 – Agree to the terms and conditions. Check that you agree to the Facebook Pages terms.

Step 7 – Select "Get Started." This will appear as a choice after you have agreed to the Facebook terms.

The second part contains the steps to filling out the information for your page and releasing it onto Facebook.

Step 1 – Add a Profile Picture – This is very important. You need a clear and professional profile picture that meets the listed criteria for Facebook images (jpg, bmp, png etc. and 64x64). Follow the options to upload a picture from your hard drive or to paste in the URL from where it is located on your website. Make sure that you click on "Save Photo" after it is uploaded.

Step 2 – Fill in the "About" section – You want this to be complete and succinct. Make sure that you put mention of your keywords and websites in the beginning of the information as this will be indexed by search engines and increase your visibility in searches. You should also add in any other social media links as well.

Step 3 – Check the type of representation – Facebook will prompt you with a question as to whether or not your fan page is for a real celebrity or a famous person. Select the appropriate answer. Keep in mind that even if you are a local celebrity, they are more concerned about national and global celebrities.

Step 4 – Save Info – This is made into its own step because a surprising amount of people forget to click this button and save all the work that they just did.

Remember: If you don't have the time or desire to do this you can easily get someone on Elance.com to set it up for you. It would probably cost less $100 for the whole Facebook set up including custom graphics designed for you.

Choosing whether to enable ads

After you save your information you will be given the option of whether or not to enable ads. These ads are your ads and they promote your pages to other people on the network. This is a great way to reach more people, but it is not free. If you want to enable the ads you will have to enter in your credit card information. It may be a good idea to wait on this to see what type of response you get using other options.

As an aside, there has been much in the news lately about Facebook making changes to how business and fan pages are organically promoted on the network. You used to be able to opt out of paying for ads and still receive promotional benefit from your page popping up in searches. This is getting to be more difficult. You want to make sure that you pay close attention to the next section to be able to generate quality likes for your page to counterbalance the loss of organic connections via the network.

Making your page stand out

Now that you have all the basics loaded in for your fan page, it is time to make it snap and jump to attract more fans. Here is a list of the things you should do to improve your page:

- Add as much information as you can
- "Like" your own page, this starts the ball rolling
- Post a status update from your personal page to promote the fan page
- Add photos. Click on the "photos" option on the fan page and select from what location you want to add them. Make sure to take advantage of tagging and titling the photos. It also helps to then repost the photos as this will lead people back to your page.
- Add a cover photo. On the right hand side of your page your will see an option to "add a cover." Click on this and choose the photo you want to upload. Make sure the photo is clear and relates to the topic of your fan page, but avoid logos and direct promotions.

Using the Admin Panel

The Admin Panel allows you to make changes to your page, promote it to increase your audience and to find help on a variety of topics. From the Admin Panel you can:

- **Edit Page** – this will let you set permissions to allow other members of your team to manage the page, change the settings on your notifications, manage users (banning and un-banning) as well as editing the information on your page.

- **Build Audience** – This option allows you to import your email contacts to send invitations to like your page, invite your Facebook friends to your page, share it on other social media networks and to create advertisements for your page. Again, the ads for your page will not be free.

- **Help** – this connects you to the forums, FAQs and Facebook Helpdesk for any problems or questions you may have about something on your page.

Adding Adwords to your Facebook Page and Fan Page

Adding Adwords to your page is easy. Follow these steps:

Step 1 - Log in to your Facebook Developer (developers.facebook.com) account and click "Set Up New Apps" from the top right corner of the window.

Step 2 - Write a name for your application, accept Facebook's terms and conditions, and then confirm your developer account with either your linked credit card or mobile phone.

Step 3 - Fill the new application form with your app's name, the intended use and category, and then click "Save Changes."

Step 4 - Click "Facebook Integration" and fill out the required fields. Copy the URL from your HTML file that contains the AdSense code and paste it into the Canvas URL field. This directs your Facebook apps to your AdSense code.

Step 5 - Click "View Apps Profile Page" then click "Add to my page" and choose which pages you would like to add the Facebook apps to. Click "Close." Return to your app's homepage and verify the AdSense ads are displayed.

How To Master Facebook Marketing Using A Unique Method
That Many So-Called 'Experts' Don't Know About!

Facebook is a giant in advertising and you can bet a large
percentage of your customers are using Facebook right now.
When customers are on Facebook they are relaxing, catching up
on family and friends and generally in a more chilled mood.

If they are looking at Facebook wouldn't it be great if you could
get you spa in front of them? A gentle reminder.

Now I don't care again if you don't like Facebook or have never used it. Your customers do, therefore you need to know how to advertise effectively to them. Go where your customers are.

This is high-end stuff and the chances are your competitors haven't even started to scratch the surface of what I'm showing you in this book. By following these methods you really can get more customers.

Most people don't know you can do this, but it can be a super powerful way of reminding your customers about your service and getting you back in front of their eyes so they remember you.

It's very simple to do - simply take your list of customer emails from Aweber and input them into Facebook.

Or if you have a few dollars go to Elance.com and get someone to set up a business page for you, claim the vanity url and create a nice Facebook header.

Here's the secret to highly targeting Facebook ads

You can actually import your customers email addresses into Facebook and give them highly targeted ads. If you want you can also advertise to their friends!

There is a great guide on exactly how to put this into action at

http://blog.wishpond.com/post/64215441993/how-to-target-facebook-ads-based-on-email-address

But remember use it creatively and you can get a great response.

You can have two lists – one of 'pre customers' where you could give them some friendly reminders about your product and great offers.

Your other 'special customers' list who have already used your service. Give them reminders, content updates and try to get repeat sales.

It's a great way of getting in front of your best audience in a non sales like way. It keeps your brand in their minds.

Making Your Local Business Mobile

Having a mobile presence isn't an option anymore it's a necessity. There are more smartphones and tablets accessing the Internet than ever before and it has replaced the yellow pages and is swiftly replacing print ads in the local business world.

Why Mobile Is Important

In a nutshell, the majority of people who use their mobile device to locate a business purchase from that business the same day. The numbers break down to over 60% of all Internet capable phone owners use their devices to find local businesses. Over 70% of those people who do are ready to buy – whether that means ordering directly through your site via their device or

166

coming to your location – that is a percentage of potential customers that you cannot ignore.

Maximize for searches or use direct apps?

The two main approaches for businesses that want to increase their mobile presence is to either focus on appearing in more mobile searches, or to use direct apps to reach customers. The fact is that neither approach is better than the other. Research has shown that the split is nearly 50/50 so you can't go wrong doing both; but you could lose 50% of your potential market if you only choose to do one.

The right mobile website

The good news is that more people than ever before are using their mobile devices, such as smartphones and tablets, to access the Internet for local business information throughout the day. What is making this possible is that the operating systems powering these devices have become able to reflect more of what is on the Internet. It used to be that unless you had a dot mobi site name, the search engines wouldn't show your site on a smartphone. Now, the search engines will return full lists.

The bad news is that just because someone can see your site on a mobile device doesn't mean that they will be able to read it or use it. Many so called "web designers" emphasize that the same designs are portable between devices and that isn't true. While users can zoom in and out of sites to view different parts of the page, the code for your buttons may not work, and their patience with doing that may not last.

A series of studies, most notably the 2011 study done by Compuware looked at the differences in behaviour and expectation that users had depending on the device they were using to access the Internet. They discovered that mobile users want sites that load fast, are easy to use and don't require any extra steps to read. If you have invested in a site full of videos, dancing widgets and pop-ups, you are going to lose a large part of the share of your local mobile market.

User expectations for mobile sites

- 71% of mobile users expect sites to load in under 2 seconds
- 57% of users won't use a business or recommend it if the mobile site is not easily used
- 40% report that one of the reasons they choose a competitor was due to their mobile site being better

What to do?

You have to make sure that your website is designed to maximize both the mobile and desktop viewer. One of the easiest ways to do this is to use responsive design. Websites that use responsive design are constructed on a grid. The code detects the size of the screen and then rearranges the grid to fit the screen. To design successfully in this manner you have to give up the static "poster" style approach to website design.

You also need to make sure of the following:

- Make sure you have fast load times by decreasing content blocks to short bullets, compressing images and linking to videos rather than embedding them.
- Create clear navigation options.

- Design your navigation features so they can be accessed from the left or right side of the screen with thumbs.
- Keep it easy to read – large buttons and dark text on a light background.
- Make sure that you don't include anything that limits the devices it will work on (such as Flash).
- Make contacting your business easy by coding it so it will trigger direct phone or texting functions on the device.
- Provide mapping location so they can easily find you.

The rule is simple to remember – mobile sites mean "a fast way to know where what you want is located and how to get there."

What mobile marketing is right for you?

Depending on who you talk to you might here that SMS marketing is the best, or just to focus on a mobile website, or that having your own app is the only way to go. The truth of the matter is that there are many different types of mobile marketing available to you. It isn't that one is better than the other, but that at different stages of your growth you will need different types of mobile marketing.

Here is an overview of the different types of mobile marketing you can do.

Custom Apps

These can help or be an enormous waste of time. It really depends on your business and what you are selling. A lot of people jumped on the bandwagon and paid to have custom apps developed for businesses that don't need one at all.

169

To determine if you need one - think of how your customers interact with your business.

If you are selling something that the customer will only need once every so often – an app doesn't make sense as they will need one set of information and then nothing else. If you have some health program to sell alongside your spa, then creating an app that provides tracking programs makes sense because it will keep your customer connected to you.

BUT – If you are a dedicated spa I would say at this stage it is not worth the cost and do not be taken in by all the fancy sales pitches. If you do want an app please get in contact as I can advise of a few good providers.

Mobile Display Ads

This can be expensive, but it can also be effective. Companies will post your ad onto other sites with real time coupons and offers that are tied to the analytics of what the person is looking at. More and more news apps are also offering this as a per-fee service to businesses to replace print advertising.

SMS Advertising

The jury is still out on the effectiveness of SMS advertising for businesses that don't have an established following. To be effective you need to have customers that are willing to sign up for the service and be able to offer them deals. This can be ideal for restaurant and entertainment venues.

Check-Ins

FourSquare and GoWalla are just two of the social networking platforms that now allow businesses a chance to pay to be a part of the options from where people can check in. While anyone can

170

say they are at your location, when you are part of the system, it will post your ad and information along with their check in. This can be a real boon for local businesses.

Fancy trying Groupon and other coupon style sites for fast customers and money?

171

Not heard of Groupon? They are basically like an online coupon site targeted for specific areas (with the added bonus that they are designed to be shared). The customer can get money off various services or free extras by going through Groupon.com.

You may think the Groupon hype is dying down a bit now and to be fair you would be partly correct. However they do have a massive list of local customers that you can potentially get access to.

You can get a quick instant boost to sales if you are accepted. However they do take a BIG percentage of the sale. So you need to ensure that it will still be profitable for you.

If you know your figures well enough and have a good follow up sequence in place and can get customers booking again perhaps you can break even or even lose on the first sale. But know your numbers before you do that.

I have heard quite a few reports of companies that have signed up to Groupon.com but after going through the promotion wouldn't do it again. Many people reported that the customers were not their natural customer and simply after a heavily discounted experience! Just go into it with your eyes open.

Their site is divided up in areas:

Featured Deal & Local
Getaways
Goods
Pets
Gifts

You'll almost certainly want to be listed in "Featured Deal & Local" You can sign up using

www.grouponworks.com

Once you have filled in the form, their marketing team will follow up and get everything set up for you.

They generally want you to offer a minimum of 50% off your normal rate and then Groupon will take about 50% on top again. So out of a $100 'normal' sale you may only make $25 and still have all your normal costs to take off.

You'll need to check these figures when Groupon contact you as there may be some negotiation on fees. Just makes sure it works for you! Groupon will put together all the sales copy to help sell the deal to their customers.

What happens?

When your deal goes live a specific number of people have to order the coupon before they all become valid. That is designed to help your offer go viral e.g. if you buy one and it says another 5 people need to order before it's live hopefully they might share the offer with their friends on Facebook, etc. The number required is decided by you and Groupon.

I would strongly suggest that you also set a maximum number of people who can claim. To make an extreme example – Say you offer a 15-minute massage and you have 500 people who claim your offer. Even if you start one massage directly after the other with absolutely no breaks you have 125 hours worth of work – almost a month's back-to-back work. All while you can't take your regular loyal and full paying customers! It can leave you overwhelmed and the result is bad online reviews.

Once someone has ordered via Groupon they can then print out the offer and contact you to make the booking.

After your offer has run Groupon then send you the money. The good thing is there is no upfront cost as Groupon take their money automatically off what they send you.

You Get Paid Regardless

Groupon also pay you regardless of if the customer ends up using the voucher. I've heard it suggested that around 20 – 30% of customers who purchase never get around to using it! You get paid for those customers!

A Few Things to Consider

You want to use Groupon to try and create long-term customer relationships. I would suggest trying to avoid a bargain 15-minute treatment. You may find you just attract bargain hunters and those never likely to return.

Could you offer 3 massages for 50% off rather than just one? Try and encourage the repeat sale. You can often put time limits and exclusions on the coupons. So you may want to limit the coupons use only for your quietest times and days. Do you really want discount users stopping you from taking full paying bookings?

Can you use them to offer the less popular treatments?

You may wish to contact some of your suppliers to see if they will help you fund the promotion. Explain to them what you are doing and since you'll be using more of their product will they contribute to the promotion. You may be surprised and unless you ask you'll never receive. Often companies have money specifically targeted for promotions.

A Few More Things to Consider

- Groupon attracts customers – People who may have never heard of your business before become aware and may use you for the first time (possibly coming away from your competitors).

- It creates awareness – Grow your brand and give customers that WOW experience so they tell their family and friends and they come back to you again and again.

- There isn't any upfront cost and it can be an easy way to generate cash.

- You can use it to fill quiet times and days – times otherwise you may have been empty or have staff not doing any treatments. Is a customer paying something better than none at all?

- Do something different that your competitors are not.

- You may get customers filling up your quiet times who would never have paid full price. They use Groupon and other offer sites with no intention of booking directly.

- It brings bargain hunters. Are the customers you gain really the customers you want? Will they ever become

175

full price paying customers? Can you do anything to make sure they are?

If you believe they will never pay full price but equally would still want them as a customer can you sell them the same offer again face to face without having to pay Groupon's share?

- Groupon want you to offer BIG discounts (it makes their site look great with offers of 80% off, etc.) but remember you still have their commission to pay on top of that. Can you operate on the margin that is left?

- Groupon don't give you the customers contact details. You need to ensure you capture these when the customer visits (you can't force them).

- Your regular full paying customers may see the offer and simply save themselves money when otherwise they would have paid full price.

- Can you deal with the extra customers and give them a quality experience?

There are other sites you can use just like Groupon

The most notable competitor is - LivingSocial (part owned by Amazon).

Others that you may wish to consider:
Amazon Local
Google Offers
Offers.com
Yelp Offers

Some Advanced Web Stuff That Can REALLY Help Make Your Site Stand Out

This is really advanced stuff that if you don't understand websites and how they work you may need to get someone to do for you.

When you've been searching the web you have probably seen some results that have included extra stuff apart from the normal title and description. These can include photos, reviews, contact details, and opening times.

If you do this right it can be VERY effective in making your listing stand out from your competition, which is why it's important that you follow the stuff I'm about to show you. Your competitors may have a website but I doubt they are using what is called

"Rich Snippets"

If your listing stands out on a page full of text because you have some nice 5 stars reviews or a few images included, where do you think a user is likely to click?

If you get the traffic you have the opportunity to make the sale that your competitors didn't. Once the customers are on your website do the other bits mentioned in this book and you should be fine. But you need to do everything possible to get visitors to click your listing.

It's Free...

Plus the good news is using 'rich snippets' is free. Search engines want you to use them as it makes it easier for them to organise your content. The easier you make it for them, the better your chances are of getting a higher listing.

Makes your listing stand out

You really want your star ratings to appear in the search engine results page. The eye is attracted to them and the number of people who click your listing should be higher than if you didn't have them. More clicks = more chances to make a sale!

Here's How To Give Yourself The Best Chance

It's thought only 1 in 300 websites are using this at the moment – so here's your chance to get a massive head start.

Google will not show rich snippets every time – even if you have everything in place that they require. It depends on a whole range of factors and they often change and test different layouts to their search pages.

179

But one thing that is important - Your website shouldn't have any errors. You can test it - validator.w3.org. If you find errors, go to Elance.com and get a programmer to fix them.

To discover more on how to use rich snippets you should visit http://schema.org. It is the definitive resource and provides lots of examples on how to correctly mark up your data.

You definitely need to use the local business function. It helps the search engines know where you are. A good signal for their local places.

You can get a detailed rich snippets guide at - http://schema.org/DaySpa

Google can help you with the code generation required for each page you want to place the rich snippets on. It's a great resource. www.google.com/webmasters/markup-helper/u/0/

Google also provide a support page at support.google.com/webmasters/answer/146750?hl=en

Once you have all your code in place make sure you test it so you know that it can be read correctly. Google provide a free tool for you to use at

www.google.com/webmasters/**tools/richsnippets**

Rich snippets can be hard to understand for anyone not familiar with web code. My best suggestion is if you don't understand it head over to Elance.com and post a project along the lines of

"I need someone who understands schema.org and rich snippets to implement it throughout my spa website.

I really need to make use of local contact details and to highlight my reviews.

You will only get paid for this job when Google starts to display the star ratings."

You can get a programming genius there to implement it for you throughout your site and it will probably only cost you a few dollars. Often that will be the quickest and cheapest way to do it.

It should pay for itself over and over again and I can't suggest how strongly I advise you to use it.

Remember Google and other search engines want to give their visitors the best possible experience (just like you) and therefore sites that help them give great content should be rewarded with higher listings.

Think of what your visitors want to see on your website. Most probably want:

- What treatments you offer
- Costs
- Online availability
- Contact details

Whilst it may be a pain for you to fully list all your treatments – do so! Give as much detail as you can (making sure it's interesting to read as well) plus use photos and more.

What's better for your customers and the search engines?

Visit www.SpaBusinessMarketing.com for MORE expert advice

- Your competitor's "30-minute full body massage, $75"

- Or your "Experience the delights of a full 30-minute totally indulgent massage…. $75 – Book online now".

That's a basic example, but whatever your competitors are doing online go one better and give your visitors a better experience.

A simple 2 page website is not as useful to Google visitors as a complete 50 page website detailing all the treatments, photos, testimonials, contact details and online booking.

What site would Google rank higher? (Higher rankings mean more chances to make a sale.) Simple – give as much quality content as you can.

You will not achieve this overnight. But start slowly and build up a quality site and add fresh content. Again Google likes sites with new content.

Summary

Running a spa is fun but hard work. However if done right it can be very, very profitable.

You really need to follow a formula that works. You'll find it helps if you can get experts to do the things you either don't have time to do or don't understand.

You are probably best to get someone else to act on all the advice given in this book (unless you want to become an expert internet marketer as well!) This stuff changes regularly and takes time to put into action – time I know is in short supply when you are running your spa.

You should focus on your strengths – the things that you provide, that are most valuable to the business and get others to do the rest.

This book is designed to be easy to read and to give you a good understanding of what online marketing needs to be done to give you a good flow of customers regularly. That way you can select the best people to help you.

We do offer a service to do ALL of what is mentioned in this book if you are interested.

Simply visit – http://www.SpaBusinessMarketing.com (you'll notice it's a squeeze page – yes we practice what we preach because it works!) Once we have your email address we can send you all the details and then you can decide if you want to use your own team or us.

Our version of your site will be designed by experts in marketing spas locally in order to give you better results and more customers.

However if you choose to do this yourself -

Here is your simple 8-step checklist of the most important elements you need to be doing right NOW!

- Get a 'responsive' website
- Give as much useful content as you possibly can
- Capture a visitor's details
- Make them a fantastic offer / trip wire
- Follow up
- Get great reviews
- Get other quality sites to promote you
- Use targeted advertising to drive customers

Good luck

PS – I Need Your Help As Well PLEASE...

Just as you need reviews, so do I. PLEASE can you take the time to leave me a review? I really would appreciate it and be very grateful. Thank you again!

185

Visit www.SpaBusinessMarketing.com for MORE expert advice

Visit www.SpaBusinessMarketing.com for MORE expert advice

Visit www.SpaBusinessMarketing.com for MORE expert advice

www.ingramcontent.com/pod-product-compliance
Lightning Source LLC
Chambersburg PA
CBHW060556200326
41521CB00007B/584